When Women Worship

GOD

AMIE DOCKERY

WITH MARY ALESSI

Regal

From Gospel Light
Ventura, California, U.S.A.

PUBLISHED BY REGAL BOOKS
FROM GOSPEL LIGHT
VENTURA, CALIFORNIA, U.S.A.
PRINTED IN THE U.S.A.

Library of Congress Cataloging-in-Publication Data
Dockery, Amie.
When women worship / Amie Dockery, Mary Alessi.
p. cm.
ISBN 0-8307-4279-4 (trade paper)
1. Women in public worship. 2. Christian women—Religious life. I. Alessi, Mary. II. Title.
BV26.7.D63 2007
264.0082—dc22   2006033136

1   2   3   4   5   6   7   8   9   10   /   10   09   08   07

Rights for publishing this book in other languages are contracted by Gospel Light Worldwide, the international nonprofit ministry of Gospel Light. Gospel Light Worldwide also provides publishing and technical assistance to international publishers dedicated to producing Sunday School and Vacation Bible School curricula and books in the languages of the world. For additional information, visit www.gospellightworldwide.org; write to Gospel Light Worldwide, P.O. Box 3875, Ventura, CA 93006; or send an e-mail to info@gospellightworldwide.org.

For Aunt Sally:
May your mantle rest on every woman
who reads this book.

"Women in general are leaders in worship—
they seem to have less inhibition."
SALLY PARKER AYERS

Amie Dockery

To my Lord and Savior, Jesus Christ, to whom my life is devoted.
I thank the Lord for the awesome privilege to use my life as an
instrument of worship unto Him.

Mary Alessi

ACKNOWLEDGMENTS

When it comes to revelation, words are powerful; but in terms of describing gratitude, they are feeble indeed! Thank you to my father for believing in God's unique anointing on women. Thank you to my husband for believing in God's unique anointing on this woman. And thank you to my mother, for living the revelation of true empowerment.

—Amie Dockery

Thank you to my awesome husband, Steve, who is a constant support and the love of my life.

To my fabulous four—my children Christopher, Stephanie, Lauren and Gabrielle: You are my inspiration.

To Amie Dockery, my friend and co-laborer in Christ: You inspire me to reach down into the deep well of revelation to hear what God is saying.

—Mary Alessi

Contents

Will you fill Him up when you feel empty?

> *His Request: To give Him the temporary*
> *Our Reward: To receive the eternal*

Will you accept what God has done to build relationship with you, and will you allow yourself to be accepted in spite of your shame?

> *His Request: To accept Him*
> *Our Reward: To be accepted*

Will you seek Him out to reveal your "secret places," or will you wait to be confronted with the truth about yourself?

> *His Request: To reveal ourselves*
> *Our Reward: To receive revelation*

Are you willing to be crushed to carry the aroma of His presence in your life?

> *His Request: A sacrificial death*
> *Our Reward: An aromatic life*

Are you prepared for the instant response required to become overshadowed?

> *His Request: No hesitation*
> *Our Reward: To be overshadowed*

What is worship? *How* do we worship? *Why* do we worship? *Who* do we worship? People have asked me these questions, and at times, I have asked them myself. After 20 years as a praise and worship leader, I thought I knew the answers; but as a result of reading *When Women Worship*, I now know that I still have much to learn. Each one of the testimonies and experiences in this book has come from a place of humility and vulnerability that is not always easy to share. Some of the women in this book have endured loss that left them devastated. Their stories have encouraged me to dig deeper into the whole subject of praise and worship and go back to where it all began.

The Bible tells us about a girl named Esther, who was able to move to a place of prominence and influence, despite her background, because she was willing to please the king. She dressed herself in the colors he liked and wore the perfume he preferred. Everything she did was about him! Because she took the time to honor the king, she had full access into his inner court and was able to save an entire nation.

In the book of Psalms, we are commanded to put on the garment of praise. We are to wrap ourselves in praise and lavish our King with worship. When we do what pleases the Lord, our God—our King—He grants us full access into His courts.

I've never felt so moved by a project as I have by the content of this book. The manifest presence of God is in its pages with the message that He is able to deliver us and set us free from past mistakes and hurts so that we can see ourselves as God sees us. We are His daughters, His baby girls, and He loves us so much, despite our failures.

If you are afraid to approach the King because of where you've come from, if you feel that your past mistakes make you unworthy to approach Him, praise Him anyway and see how He meets you in that place.

What is worship, and how do we worship? Why do we worship, and who is it that we worship? The testimonies in this book will take you deeper and give you greater insight to answer these questions. As you read the remarkable testimonies here, my prayer is that you will see for yourself the transforming power that is released when women worship.

Martha Munizzi
Songwriter and Worship Leader

Purchasing a gift can be an unnerving experience, especially if I'm not sure what I'm looking for. Watching someone open a gift that was purchased under such circumstances is even more stressful than the shopping! I find myself thinking, *What if I'm way off base and I've missed it altogether?*

Maybe I overthink it a bit (I do tend to overthink most everything, at least a little). But when I buy someone a gift, I want that person to feel understood and appreciated. I wouldn't want to give someone a gift that wasn't a reflection of his or her personal taste, desires and personality. So when I'm sure I have picked up on the person's hints, and I'm on the right track to what they would like, then it's exciting to go shopping! And it's rewarding to watch the gift being opened. I'm sure you will agree that the joy of giving is even greater when you know that you are fulfilling someone else's desire!

I happen to know what God desires as a gift. He wants *you*—the real, authentic version. He wants all of you, the whole package. How do I know? Psalm 51:6 tells us, "Surely you desire truth in the inner parts; you teach me wisdom in the inmost place."

How many of us would spend all of our time and money on the gift wrap, while giving little or no thought to the gift itself? And yet when we think of worship, we spend most of our time examining the outward presentation or demonstration, while completely forgetting to reflect on the treasure within. The "gift wrap" has taken priority over the gift!

I fear that our focus on talent in relation to worship has undermined the divine exchange that worship is designed to orchestrate for every believer. In fact, I would venture to guess that many believers don't see themselves as worshipers because their assumption is based solely upon the outward challenge of expressing themselves. Although worship is an expression of what is on the inside, worship is not the ability to "perform" vocally. My friend and coauthor, Mary Alessi, is in complete agreement that there has been a problem with perspective regarding worship. Although there is much attention given to the outward demonstration, there is little acknowledgment of the internal preparation and response. Worship, however, is so much more than a song or dance; it is the atmosphere we prepare and the connection we share. It has everything to do with our desperate need for God and His boundless love for us.

If we can worship in spirit and truth as Jesus instructed us to do, then we will have communion with God. And if we can commune with Him, we will be endowed with power, equipped with authority, and enabled by His grace to restore a fallen world.

The Spirit of God is hovering today, seeking true worshipers who can conceive the prophetic future of the Kingdom. I believe that women are uniquely designed by God to host the work of the Holy Spirit. This process is not "one size fits all"; it is a unique, divine exchange that takes place when one embraces the decision to give Him everything.

My prayer is that women all over the world will begin to recognize their place in the kingdom of God, as well as recognize the devil's diabolical plan to keep them from fruitfulness. Women have been the most oppressed people group throughout history, and yet God has chosen to esteem women by using them to produce His will on Earth. I pray that you will join other women throughout history on this intimate journey toward deeper relationship with our Maker. He is waiting—and the world is waiting. As you read these pages, may you withhold nothing in your pursuit of the Lover of your soul!

Amie Dockery

"Willing"

O God, you are my God, earnestly I seek you;
my soul thirsts for you, my body longs for you, in a dry
and weary land where there is no water.

PSALM 63:1

Mary Ann had lived in the desert her entire life. Born and raised in an arid land where the nearly constant hum of air conditioners was just part of the lifestyle, and the family refrigerator was always well stocked with cold drinks, she gave little thought to the importance of life-sustaining water—until one very hot August day when both her nearly new sports car and her state-of-the-art cell phone failed her at the same time.

Miles from home—and from any other part of civilization—Mary Ann fought her rising sense of panic as she reassured herself that she had plenty of water in the trunk of her car. But when she popped the latch and looked inside, the five-gallon container of water that her father insisted she carry with her at all times was missing. She immediately remembered what had happened just two days earlier, when she met a friend in need on her way into town. Tony's car had broken down by the side of the road. He said he needed water to get it running again, so Mary Ann gave him the container from her trunk, assuring him that she would replace it as soon as she got home.

Obviously, she had forgotten. And now here she was, her own car refusing to go another mile and her cell phone unable to pick up a signal. As she gazed down the road, first in one direction and then the other, the vastness of the landscape and the improbability of another motorist coming along anytime soon seemed to intensify the 115-degree heat that threatened to suffocate her.

If only she had listened to her father's advice about sticking to the main roads; but she'd been taking short-cuts through the desert since she'd first received her driver's license three years earlier, and never before had she run into a problem. After all, her car was in excellent condition, and there were very few areas where her cell phone didn't work. She wondered how it was possible that both the car and the phone would give out on her at the exact same time she happened to be out on a lonely, deserted road without her usual reserve of drinking water—but there she was, and the temperature wouldn't drop for several hours yet.

The very thought caused her throat to tickle and her tongue to thicken. How long could she last out here without water? How long until someone found her—dead or alive? She'd heard that dehydration was one of the most cruel and agonizing deaths imaginable. The more she thought about it, the more frightened she became, and the more she longed for just one cool, clear drink of water.

A small sliver of shade from her car was the only spot she could find to get any respite from the merciless sun. As she sat in the dirt beside the road and leaned her back against the front fender, she told herself she didn't dare fall asleep in case there were poisonous snakes or scorpions nearby. And yet she must have nodded off, for the last thing she remembered was asking God to protect her and to please send help—and the next thing she knew, someone was shaking her awake.

"Are you okay?" a voice demanded.

Mary Ann opened her eyes to see the grizzled features of a bearded old man staring down at her, concern mirrored in his rheumy eyes as he offered her a canteen. When he smiled, she noticed that most of his teeth were missing; but Mary Ann thought he was the most hand-some man she had ever seen as she opened her cracked, dry lips to receive the life-giving liquid.

As it turned out, Mary Ann had been stranded for less than two hours before the elderly gentleman came along, but as she gulped the refreshing water, she was sure she had been out in the heat for an eternity. When she was able to talk, she thanked the man for stopping to help her, and she vowed never again to take such foolish chances and cut herself off from the water that is so vital for sustaining life.

Many things draw us to desire and seek more of God. In times of tragedy or desperation, we search for the hand and heart of our Creator. I (Amie) have often wondered that if it weren't for the needs in our lives, would we ever look to the sky with longing? And further, is it possible to pierce the deep waters of the Spirit without the upheaval of the dry, hard exterior of our lives?

The desire for union with God is deep within us all, but most often forgotten in times of bounty. Two things clearly drive our thirst for more water: a wilderness experience and a day of hard labor. Those who are in a spiritual desert are clearly desperate for relief that only the Spirit of God can quench. In this case, lack drives our desire. The other extreme that sets us on a search for more is when we are giving out, as laborers in the harvest field. When we're busy pouring ourselves into the lives of others, we create a great need for access to a deep well—not for ourselves alone, but for those whom we are watering.

It is between those who are "lacking" and those who are "laboring" that we find everyone else, the "seemingly satisfied"—those who have been watered and raised by laborers who, on their behalf, go to the well of worship for them. Although this is a necessary step in the road to spiritual growth, it is not a permanent solution. There will come a time when the longing of those "in between" will no longer be satisfied by water from someone else's well. And unless they take their great thirst and focus it on digging their own well of worship, they will be driven into the desert where their desire will turn to desperation and, ultimately, to a battle for spiritual survival.

You may even now find yourself in the dry heat of your own desert, where you have never been so sure that you needed the water of refreshment. Or you may be a laborer in need of a deeper well to sustain the bounty of God's favor in your life. You may even be a zealous, growing young sprout, licking up every drop around you. Wherever you find yourself in this circle of thirst, there is only a short span of time when you will be satisfied with a sprinkling of water. When you are new, when you are small, it takes only a few drops to soak you—body, soul and spirit. But as you grow, you will ache for more, and your great thirst for more of God is what brings you to the well of worship.

In the fall of 2004, my well was running dry. The drought had been a process brought on in the spring of 2003 by the knowledge that my Aunt Sally, my mother's only sister, had a brain tumor. Initially, in the heat of the trial, I was ever so grateful for the well of worship I had dug out years before when my brother was hit by a car. I knew intimately the depth of excavation endured and the joy springing forth as a result. As a church family, we had long celebrated the phenomenal miracle of healing that my brother had experienced, and as a result of the trial, we were all changed for the better.

Since that time, I hadn't bothered to dig any deeper, as I was living off the abundance of that breakthrough. But when it came to dealing with the terminal prognosis of my beloved aunt, my well seemed shallow after all. The battle was longer and more tiresome, and I began to realize that I was in danger of hitting bottom. I needed a deeper well.

Drawn to a Deeper Place

My Aunt Sally was not only family, but she was also—along with her husband—the pastor of our music ministry and our worship leader at church. I had never known Aunt Sally as anything other than a dynamic singer and a passionate worshiper. She and my mother and one of their brothers had been singing together in church since they were children. Their dedication to worship grew out of their lifestyle and into a music ministry that touched the world. I had always known that my mother and her sister and brother had been all over the world before I was born, and my cousins and I often sat around and listened to our parents' old records and longed for the passion they possessed.

My aunt, in particular, never just sang a song—she preached it! She felt and expressed the heart of worship with every note. So when this devastating cancer in her brain stole her ability to read and then to sing, muddy water from my well just wouldn't satisfy the need. It was time to dig deeper, to see the Holy Spirit's presence in a more profound way.

In October 2004, I started to dig again. For 40 days, more than 200 women joined together in this endeavor of consecrated worship, fasting and prayer. As a result of the experience, we collectively hit an underground river. It was during this time that I witnessed the deepest level of worship I had ever seen. My Aunt Sally, no longer able to sing, sat in a wheelchair before a crowd of several thousand roaring worshipers, and shouted, "Worship Him! Worship! Worship!" With her hands thrown in the air, she exhorted us to press in deeper.

There are scarcely any words to describe what I felt that day. I watched the woman who had been my teacher— a woman with perfect pitch and unparalleled talent, who had challenged me to sing and worship with excellence— demonstrate that real worship can't be lost in the illusion of our ability. Aunt Sally modeled to all of us that true worship lies in the depth of our need of and gratitude for the Almighty. Our thirst, our desperation to dig, produces a well where His reflection can be found.

On December 23, 2004, my dear Aunt Sally went to be with the Lord. Although our prayer, fasting and worship had not changed the ultimate plan of God for my aunt, it had changed us. In fact, the book you now hold in your hand is a direct result of the divine exchange reaped during that season of worship in my life.

Although many things bring us closer to God, our needs are what bind us to desire Him in our lives and to pursue Him through worship. There was a response from heaven during our time of consecration regarding my aunt. She moved from a place of sadness and depression over her illness to a place of power and passion. Although she had been a talented worshiper and singer before the tumor progressed, toward the end of her life, she remained a passionate worshiper in spite of her inability to sing. Aunt Sally's need for healing became a catalyst that drew me to a deeper place.

More

MARY ALESSI

Think how you would feel if you took your child to the toy store and said, "Buy something you like," and your child replied, "Mother, I don't need anything else. You've done so much for me already; I'm just happy being here with you." Every parent would agree that your child must be the most sensitive, wonderful child on Earth. You would then insist on giving the child something, even if you had to pick it out yourself. After all, an attitude like that should be rewarded.

Unlike that perfect, imaginary child, however, we often get caught up in the quest for more, only to find ourselves asking for more of the wrong things. Material possessions are great, but there is so much more to God than the physical blessings He can provide. The inward work of the Holy Spirit is

the most valuable possession we can attain. Does God really know how much more we need and desire Him over the immediate answer to our prayers, or have we put our "needs" in front of our desire for more of Him? Do we spend most of our time in worship buttering Him up for the big questions, or do we see worship as an opportunity to express our deepest love and gratitude for who He is rather than for what He gives?

More of God's presence is what we should be seeking when given an audience with the Most High—even as Queen Esther requested more time from the king instead of bombarding him with her urgent need. She took her time feeding and entertaining the king, making him welcome in her chamber, before she made her request known. In fact, as it turned out, she didn't even have to bring up her need. Because she had focused her energy on giving to the king, he offered her anything she wanted in return, saying that nothing would be withheld from her. When *knowing* the King of kings matters more to us than *receiving* from Him, He will not withhold any good thing from us.

I Thirst for You

If it were not for the personal, everyday needs of life, perhaps we would never know the magnitude of our true need for God. There are many women of the Bible who pressed through to a deeper level in their relationship with the living God because of their need for something. Mary of Bethany, who is known for breaking her extravagant alabaster jar of perfume and pouring out its contents on the feet of Jesus (see Mark 14:1-11; John 12:1-11), was driven by her need for expression; Hannah's need for fulfillment in having a child drove her to public weeping on the steps of the tabernacle; Ruth's need for completion set her resolve to follow her mother-in-law, Naomi, without any promise for a future.

Like the Samaritan woman who went to draw water from a well and met Jesus there, our own practical needs may also lead us to a meeting place with the Almighty. The question is, When you come to this place of need at the well of living water, will you be surprised if God asks something of you first?

> When a Samaritan woman came to draw water, Jesus said to her, "Will you give me a drink?"
> The Samaritan woman said to him, "You are a Jew and I am a Samaritan woman. How can you ask me for a drink?" (For Jews do not associate with Samaritans.) (John 4:7,9).

Have you ever come to the well, longing to be filled, and before you extract your blessing, you hear the words of requirement ringing in your ears, *"Will you give me . . . ?"* That has happened to me, and my initial reaction is almost always, "But I'm empty. That's why I'm here, Lord . . . to be filled by You." And like the Samaritan woman, I respond, "How could *You* ask *me*?"

The Jews did not associate with the Samaritans, because they considered themselves God's chosen people, while they believed the Samaritans to be a mongrel race. In addition, this particular woman was considered an immoral outcast by the very Samaritans among whom she lived. Not only was she considered cursed because she was barren, but she also had been married and divorced several times and now lived with a man to whom she wasn't married. This woman was such an outcast among her people that she couldn't even come to the well to draw water in the cool of the morning or evening when the other women were there; she had to wait and come during the heat of the day when the "respectable" women were at home. It is therefore easy to understand why she responded to Jesus, a Jewish man, in much the same way we would respond to God if He asked us for something: "How could You need anything from me?"

Certainly, if Jesus had wanted water, He could get it without asking a lowly woman for it. This scenario, therefore, raises the following questions: First, why would Jesus put Himself in a position to "need" something from this Samaritan woman? Second, why would God put Himself in a position to need something from you and me?

It seems clear that Jesus *wanted* to need her, just as He wants to need us. If the Samaritan woman had known Jesus and His nature, she probably would have been more than willing to fill Him up first, before asking Him to fill her:

> Jesus answered her, "If you knew the gift of God and who it is that asks you for a drink, you would have asked him and he would have given you living water" (John 4:10).

The gift of God is the eternal reward of relationship with our Maker. The Samaritan woman offering water to Jesus is a picture of how we can offer ourselves and all we have to Him as a living sacrifice (see Rom. 12:1). But ultimately, it cannot compare to our being filled and saturated by the Spirit of God, a gift that lasts forever. We are blessed to see a glimpse of God's intentions toward us through the dialogue Jesus had with the woman at the well. The recounting of this incident was not written for our entertainment, but rather for our education in the knowledge of the nature of God, which seeks always to give us good things.

Jesus answered, "Everyone who drinks this water will be thirsty again, but whoever drinks the water I give him will never thirst. Indeed, the water I give him will become in him a spring of water welling up to eternal life" (John 4:13-14).

As Jesus said, when we drink earthly water to fill our temporal physical need, we will be thirsty again. But when we begin to search for true fulfillment, He will find us dipping our bucket and invite us to go deeper, far beyond the meeting of our temporal need to a place of everlasting relationship.

Where There's a Will, There's a Well

MARY ALESSI

I was raised as a pastor's daughter and have now served as a pastor myself for more than 15 years. As such, I have been privileged to hear many amazing life stories.

One story that struck a deep chord with me was about a lovely young lady in our church whose name is Jennifer. This dear girl had suffered great tragedy early in her life. At the age of 16, her mother had a momentary lapse in judg-

ment and committed a crime that resulted in her being sentenced to serve between 5 and 8 years in the state penitentiary. Jennifer was then left with the responsibility of raising her two brothers, a job for which she was not prepared. But Jennifer was not your typical 16-year-old. She rose to the challenge and now, at the age of 20, has become one of the most mature young women I have ever known. Jennifer and her brothers have flourished over the past four years and now look forward to their mother's release this Christmas.

As my husband and I had dinner with Jennifer one night, she began to tell us that she needed parents in her life to give her direction and guidance, because she felt that God was calling her into full-time ministry, but she didn't know what to do or where to start.

Immediately my husband began to encourage her. "Jennifer, this is your moment. God wants to use your story to minister to young women everywhere. You have a strong will to serve God, and where there's a will, there's a way—and God will provide it."

When my husband said those words, the Spirit of the Lord rose up in me and said, "Tell her, where there's a *will*, there's a *well*. Whatever she needs, if she has the will to ask, I will provide a well of resource for her."

Jesus said, "I do not seek My own will but the will of the Father who sent Me" (John 5:30, *NKJV*). Many of us know our own will but may feel distant from the knowledge of God's will for our lives. If we are willing, God will make sure there is a resource available to us to help deal with the emotions of our flesh. He knows us better than we know ourselves, and He will not manipulate or control our free will; but if we release our will to Him, He will provide a well of resources to us.

A will denotes determination; a well denotes depth. Where there is determination (a will) to serve God, there is a depth provided to do it well.

If we have the will to fight, God provides the well. His Word says that no weapon formed against us will prosper (see Isa. 54:17).

If we have the will to wait and be patient, He provides the well. His Word says to let patience have its perfect work (see Jas. 1:4).

If we have the will to desire more in the area of our finances, He provides a well. His Word says that He gives seed to the sower (see 2 Cor. 9:10).

A willing heart is determined to dig deep and know that God is our resource and our supply. Willingness is crucial to God, because it reinforces the authenticity of our worship—that we are offering up our lives without argument, debate or negotiation. When we seek the Father's will and not our own, we worship from our spirit. His will is not accomplished by what we achieve *for* Him; it's accomplished by who we are *in* Him.

We can have everything we want—*if He is all we need!*

The woman at the well left her water pot behind after her encounter with Jesus. The need that brought her to the well was irrelevant once she had been filled with the revelation of His will. Everything we could ever desire is there waiting for us if we will surrender our will to God. When we first received Jesus as Savior, we made the initial relinquishment of our hearts to God; now it's time to dig the well and go deeper.

Be willing to let God have everything so that He can show you what He's capable of doing in you and for you. Go deep in Him!

Sacred Expression

1. Like the woman at the well, have you experienced a private meeting with God?
2. Which well of worship do you frequent more— private time or public gathering?
3. What need or circumstance drove you to go deeper in God?
4. Have you been in a wilderness experience or in a season of labor that has caused you to need more from God?
5. In what area of your life have you suffered barrenness?
6. When you dug deeper to get more of God, did you find that you received something even greater than what you hoped for?

7. Have you ever heard the voice of God asking for something from you?
8. What have you done to show God that you are willing to release what you have to give?

The Divine Exchange

His Request: To give Him the temporary
Our Reward: To receive the eternal

- Jesus asked the woman for *water*.
- Her water would meet His *physical* need.
- Jesus offered her *living* water.
- His water would meet her *spiritual* need.
- If we are *willing* to fill Him up even when we feel *empty* . . . worship offers us the same divine exchange.
- We give Him *the temporary*.
- We receive *the eternal*.

Meet a Modern-Day Woman of Worship
Nicole Binion: "Willing"

Nicole Binion is one of those singers who make every song sound as if you are hearing it for the very first time. Her musical versatility is astounding. One minute she is raspy and airy, and the next moment she is belting out a song with crystal-clear tone. She is a one-of-a-kind singer. And yet, what is truly astounding about Nicole is her humility and purity—she seems unaware of the depth of her talent and ability. What is also shocking is that more people don't know her name. Upon hearing her sing, your first thought is, *This girl can be as big as she wants to be!*

As a child, Nicole had similar thoughts about her life. She had aspirations to one day be like Barbra Streisand and other great female legends of song. And she was well on her way. Those who heard her sing in church when she was 12 years old have said she was blowing away crowds even then. And though her voice grew stronger with age, she was the essence at 12 of what she is today. As she matured and the path of her life began to take its course, she saw the hand of God taking her away from her dream of fame.

The most dramatic turn in the road came when she realized who it was that she would marry. After graduating from high school, she married David Binion, a renowned worship leader who had also been singing and writing songs from a young age. When Nicole and David married, their lives, ministries and passions came together as well. They began to travel together, ministering in the greatest revivals and meetings of our generation.

Nicole has never questioned or regretted her decision to pursue God's dream for her over her own plan for success. Her willingness to give up her own desire has caused a multiplication in her passion, anointing and effectiveness as a minister of music. In recent days, David and Nicole have had trouble keeping up with the abundance of favor and resource God has sent their way. The Bible tells us that our sacrificial living comes before Him as a sweet aroma—and then He remembers us. Keeping that in mind, we are more likely remembered by God for what we have *willingly* given to Him, not for what He has given us.

"Accepted"

To the praise of the glory of His grace, by which
he made us accepted in the Beloved.

EPHESIANS 1:6, *NKJV*

Jenna's parents were killed in an automobile accident when she was two. She lived with three sets of foster parents before she was five. Finally, just before she started kindergarten, she was adopted by a lovely Christian couple who told her how very much they loved her and how happy they were to have her as their daughter.

But Jenna was afraid. Each time she loved someone, that person disappeared—and she never knew why, though she was sure it had something to do with her being a bad girl. If only she could be really, really good, then maybe this new mom and dad wouldn't disappear like the others.

When Jenna was chosen to play the part of one of the ballerinas in the school play, she was sure this was the test.

If she was a very, very good ballerina, her parents would keep her, but if she failed . . .

Jenna tried not to think about what would happen if she failed. Instead she tried very, very hard to be the best dancer in the entire play. She practiced and practiced, but the closer it got to the evening of the play, the more nervous she became, and her movements became more and more wooden and stiff. Her teacher told her time and again to relax, and she tried very hard to do that, but the harder she tried, the more she failed. By the time the curtain was raised on the performance, and Jenna spotted her newest set of parents anxiously watching her from the front row, she realized it was hopeless. By the end of the evening, she would once again be alone, and it took all the strength she had just to keep from crying as she did the very best she could to dance with the other ballerinas.

And then it was over. As the audience applauded and cheered, Jenna dared to look out at those two special people in the front row only to see them jump to their feet, clapping wildly and calling, "Bravo! Bravo, Jenna!"

That's when the astonished little girl stopped holding back. She let the tears flow as she ran from the stage right into the waiting arms of her very own parents. "You were wonderful, Jenna!" they said, hugging and kissing her and reassuring her of their love. "We are so very proud of you! You did a wonderful job."

Jenna was only five, but she was old enough to know that she had not done a wonderful job at all—and yet these two people who called themselves her mom and dad seemed to think she had. At that moment, she knew they were not going to disappear like the others. They loved her no matter what—she belonged to them, and they were her family.

Love flourishes in an atmosphere of acceptance, whether love between children and parents or between a shepherd king and his lover.

Worship Begins with Love

The Song of Songs (or Song of Solomon, as it is sometimes called) is a unique book of the Bible. It is an elaborate, descriptive story of a shepherd king—the lover—and his beloved. There are many theological opinions on the subject of this particular book, but one widely accepted viewpoint is that it is an allegory of God's love for His people.

What is overwhelmingly felt as one reads this book is the deep longing of the back-and-forth dance between two lovers. Though the story is interspersed with crowds and public displays, the primary focus of the text is on the private exchanges that occur in and around the public celebration.

When I read the story of the Song of Songs, I personally make the connection to my own attendance at public gatherings of worship where I still feel as though my worship is privately celebrated and acknowledged by God. Even in the midst of a great multitude, He knows that I am present, and He hears every word I say and every phrase I sing as if I'm whispering them in His ear.

Worship always begins with wonder as we express our delight for the pleasing nature and goodness of God. It is the kiss of heaven, the affection of the King for which we so desperately long. It is not only His presence that we seek but also His acceptance—His embrace.

> Let him kiss me with the kisses of his mouth—for your love is more delightful than wine.
>
> Pleasing is the fragrance of your perfumes; your name is like perfume poured out. No wonder the maidens love you!
>
> Take me away with you—let us hurry! Let the king bring me into his chambers (Song of Songs 1:2-4)

When we are caught up in worship, we hope to move to a deeper place with haste, before we lose the sensation of the moment. But how often do we linger in His presence long enough to accept His gaze? Are we comfortable in the place of worship only when the focus is on God?

No one but you knows what thoughts arise in your mind when the subject of worship comes up. Although there are many images today of what worship represents, there is only one definition to focus on—yours—because whatever you believe worship to be will determine how you relate to God.

Worship as a lifting of the hands or a yielding of the heart or a dancing of the feet is a feeble portrait when compared to the image of everything worship must come to mean in our lives. Although worship includes the lifting of hands, the yielding of hearts and the dancing of feet—and must also be put into words—it is not restricted or confined to any one of these alone. Rather, worship is everything together. The "everything" is the captured essence of worship, not the expression we choose to display on the face of our worship. Simply put, *worship is focusing everything I am on everything He is.* That may sound simple enough, but this kind of focus requires us to look into His eyes without tipping our chin downward or turning our face away.

"Show Me Your Face"

Let's look back at the Song of Songs, where the shepherd king—the lover—is calling to his beloved.

> My dove in the clefts of the rock, in the hiding places on the mountainside, show me your face, let me hear your voice; for your voice is sweet, and your face is lovely (2:14).

Many lovers of God come into His presence just long enough to express their gratitude and to experience the good feeling, but not long enough for Him to set His eyes upon them. How many of us are comfortable with worship as long as it is about God? But the moment His gaze is drawn to us, we respond defensively! Let us see how quickly she—the beloved—turned to defend her "darkness," even giving a good reason for her exposure to the sun.

> Do not stare at me because I am dark, because I am darkened by the sun. My mother's sons were angry with me and made me take care of the vineyards; my own vineyard I have neglected.
> Tell me, you whom I love, where you graze your flock and where you rest your sheep at mid-

day. Why should I be like a veiled woman beside the flocks of your friends? (1:6-7).

The beloved did not trust that the king was staring at her because he loved what he saw. Instead, she assumed that he was rejecting her. As a result, she responded ignorantly.

At that point in history, a pale complexion was considered the standard of beauty (only recently has a tan been considered to enhance a woman's good looks). It was previously considered undesirable to be a woman with a tanned complexion, since tanned skin indicated that she had been exposed to the hard life, working outside in the elements. Pale skin denoted a woman who had been highborn to a life of leisure. Therefore, if a woman had a tan, she was immediately known as a woman who had to labor in order to survive in a harsh environment. The beloved was one of these women who, although very beautiful, had reason to turn her suntanned face in shame.

Since the fall of humankind, we have run in shame from the God who loves us. From that fateful moment in the Garden, it seems to be our nature to deem ourselves unworthy, imperfect. Why do we seem to prefer to judge and reject ourselves rather than await God's response? Although we are not perfect, who are we to assume that our King will not find us beautiful?

When the beloved asked her questions of the king, she did not really want an answer—she wanted unconditional acceptance, something she would not find among her friends, as we see when they speak to her in 1:8.

> If you do not know, most beautiful of women, follow the tracks of the sheep and graze your young goats by the tents of the shepherds.

As is common with well-meaning friends, they begin to tell her all the things she could have done differently. We must never measure God's feelings toward us by the acceptance or rejection we experience in our human relationships. God's ways are not taken from the judgment of men. Our opinion should be taken from the order of the Highest Court, for it is only the King's thoughts and ways that should decide our destiny.

> "For my thoughts are not your thoughts, neither are your ways my ways," declares the LORD. "As the heavens are higher than the earth, so are my ways higher than your ways and my thoughts than your thoughts" (Isa. 55:8-9).

More Than Just a Man

All women long to be loved and accepted in a lavish and unconditional fashion. Because of this deep longing, just being a woman changes the very nature of worshiping a God who reveals Himself as God the Father. As little girls, we first look for love in the eyes of our father, and later in the arms of a lover. However, both of these relationships are, at best, a dim reflection of the love our King has for us.

When women worship, they are always aware of their femininity in relationship to their heavenly Father. Our femininity may be a hindrance in itself if we liken God to every man in our lives. We are daughters, wives, mothers and sisters to males, and each of these relationships has its own complicated issues. So as our dream of flawless love begins to fade, we may find ourselves responding to God in the same way we might respond to a man made of flesh. And that is a grievous mistake, for although God primarily reveals Himself in masculine metaphors, He is not a man. As women, we must release all of the negative reactions we may have to the masculine side of God because a defensive attitude will ultimately render our worship sterile and unproductive.

The very nature of being feminine should enable us to see God as the Lover of our soul. But because of shame, our nature tends to work against us. As a result, both His identity and ours are falsified in our eyes. We then prejudge the boundaries of acceptance based upon our feelings of rejection. (I am sure that men would have their own issues with this if God were primarily portrayed as a woman—men would then have to overcome patterns of relationship they have had with women in order to see God unhindered by earthly concepts of human relationships.)

If we, as women, see ourselves as unworthy to enter into the presence of God, then we will never push through the illusions of the enemy. The Word of God is the most revealing tool we possess as we seek to understand the true heart of God toward women. This is best done using the Word of God as testimony to the love, understanding and commitment God has for womankind.

Knowing of the hatred, mistreatment and bondage that women suffered during biblical times, it is clearly evident that the inclusion of liberating stories about women in the Bible was deliberately orchestrated by God. Our loving Father wanted each profound story to illustrate His affection for women.

We will have peace in God's presence when we arrive at the knowledge that God desires us to come freely to Him, uninhibited in our affection. His expectation is not that we come to Him completely whole, but that we come to Him with complete abandon, wholly acceptable, just as we are.

Come Boldly Before the Throne

MARY ALESSI

During their years in the wilderness, the children of Israel worshiped God in the Tabernacle. This portable place of worship consisted of a large courtyard with two inner chambers—the Holy Place and the Most Holy Place—each leading deeper inside toward the manifest presence of God. The innermost room was a small dark place where the High Priest met with God once every year on Yom Kippur—the Day of Atonement, the most holy day on the Jewish calendar—in order to make atonement for the sins of the people. As the children of Israel anxiously waited outside the Tabernacle, the High Priest entered the Most Holy Place with a cup full of the blood of an innocent animal. His mission was to lift the densely crafted veil and slip underneath it into the place of meeting with God. He would then pour out the blood upon the Mercy Seat. Then he waited for God to respond.

When the blood and the priest had been found acceptable, the Spirit of God would shine, filling the room with light. There was no other source of light in the Most Holy Place, for God wanted the priest to experience complete darkness as a symbol of the sinful condition of humankind as well as humankind's inability to save itself. Only the High Priest was allowed behind the veil, and every year he would carry out the same ritual of covering the sin of the people with innocent blood, pushing judgment another year into the future.

When Jesus Christ came to Earth, He fulfilled every duty of the High Priest of Israel. He died as the spotless, sacrificial lamb. He poured out His own blood, covering our sin forever. And He ripped the veil in two—from top to bottom—so that we could freely enter into His presence at all times.

"And when Jesus had cried out again in a loud voice, he gave up his spirit. At that moment the curtain of the temple was torn in two from top to bottom" (Matt. 27:50-51).

This symbolic gesture shows us God's desire for us to have nothing keeping us from a clear view of His presence. He wants to move freely among us. On that great Day of Atonement, when the blood of the perfect Lamb of God was shed for the sins of the world, our pardon was granted. Jesus made a way for us—once and for all—to come boldly before His throne.

"Therefore, since we have a great high priest who has gone through the heavens, Jesus the Son of God, let us hold firmly to the faith we profess. For we do not have a high priest who is unable to sympathize with our weaknesses, but

we have one who has been tempted in every way, just as we are—yet was without sin. Let us then approach the throne of grace with confidence, so that we may receive mercy and find grace to help us in our time of need" (Heb. 4:14-16).

We as women must find the courage to overcome any obstacle to authentic worship by identifying and uprooting the sources of shame. Unless we take this initial step, we cannot journey toward transparent, real relationship through worship.

You cannot reject the acceptance of the King unless you turn your face from Him. Let Him look at you right now. Don't be ashamed to let His face shine upon your darkness. Let nothing keep you from the favor of His gaze.

> The LORD make his face shine upon you and be gracious to you; the LORD turn his face toward you and give you peace (Num. 6:25-26).

In the Song of Songs, the king blesses the beloved with his true feelings about her tanned beauty. He responds to her feelings of shame by reaffirming in detail the beautiful, unique features of her appearance.

I liken you, my darling, to a mare harnessed to one of the chariots of Pharaoh. Your cheeks are beautiful with earrings, your neck with strings of jewels. How beautiful you are, my darling! Oh, how beautiful! Your eyes are doves (1:9-10,15).

It is just like God to remind us of how He feels about us. Like the beloved who had been exposed to the sun, we, in spite of our own exposure to shameful experiences, have no need to explain or defend the results in our lives. Shame is a result of this sinful world, and our exposure to it has affected our feelings of acceptance in the presence of God.

The wear and tear of life is as obvious to God as a suntan would be to the lover in the Song of Songs. The Lord knows what has caused us to feel shame. We may have fallen victim to abuse, divorce or disappointment in our lives, leaving us feeling ashamed. The beloved in the Song of Songs couldn't have done anything to keep the sun from shining on her and tanning her skin, just as we can't always control those things that cause us to feel like covering our faces with our hands. Yet when we bask in the presence of the Lord, we have no need to hide our faces anymore.

Those who look to him are radiant; their faces are
never covered with shame (Ps. 34:5).

Worship creates an environment in which the damage of sin can be reversed. Adam and Eve, acting out of
the shame of their sin, shunned the presence of God. But
if we accept the price that Jesus paid when He hung on
the cross, then our sin is no longer an issue. We are free
to pursue relationship with God—which we must active-
ly do—because only His presence will undo shame in our
lives. Although shame is understandable, it is not an
acceptable or honorable response to One who so clearly
loves and accepts us. It is our duty to release the imperfect vision we have of ourselves and embrace the opinion
of our King.

The king is enthralled by your beauty; honor him,
for he is your lord (Ps. 45:11).

He Offers Complete Security

After the beloved is assured of her lover's affection for
her, she again praises him, and he responds by describing
the security of the home that he offers her.

The beams of our house are cedars; our rafters are firs (Song of Songs 1:17).

It might seem odd for him to mention the structure of a home as a response to her admiration. But if you are a woman considering marriage, it is important to feel that you are entering a place of security, that your groom has made special preparations for the covenant of marriage to take place. He must be willing to become your provider. The best candidates would certainly have a job, a car, a house and preferably no debt. In biblical times the groom would spend one entire year building a home in which he and his betrothed would live. This shelter represented his sacrifice and his willingness to provide a place for their relationship to become established.

It is the same with God. He is our heavenly Provider, the perfect Groom who has given all to prepare a place for us.

Find rest, O my soul, in God alone; my hope comes from him. He alone is my rock and my salvation; he is my fortress, I will not be shaken. My salvation and my honor depend on God; he is my mighty rock, my refuge. Trust in him at all times,

O people; pour out your hearts to him, for God is our refuge (Ps. 62:5-8).

God is a rock, a refuge and a shelter, and He has already paid a great price to prepare a place where we can live with Him forever.

There is a reward that awaits God's people, but we must accept it. Worship opens the door so that we can receive that reward, and grace draws us in to where He dwells.

Therefore, since we are receiving a kingdom that cannot be shaken, let us be thankful, and so worship God acceptably with reverence and awe, for our "God is a consuming fire" (Heb. 12:28-29).

He has lovingly built us a permanent home for our hearts, made from the beams of a cross and painted scarlet with the blood of His great sacrifice.

How lovely is your dwelling place, O LORD Almighty! My soul yearns, even faints, for the courts of the LORD; my heart and my flesh cry out for the living God. Even the sparrow has found a home, and the swallow a nest for herself, where she may

have her young—a place near your altar, O LORD
Almighty, my King and my God. Blessed are those
who dwell in your house; they are ever praising you
(Ps. 84:1-4).

After everything God has done to bring us into a
place of communion with Him, how could we ever imagine we would not be welcomed there?

I Am Always Welcome

MARY ALESSI

Feeling unwelcome is one of the worst of human experiences. It is almost unbearable to walk into an environment that seems indifferent to our presence, and even
worse to be completely ignored or rejected. Some people
feel this way when they walk into a church setting. Even
before they arrive, they have convinced themselves that
they're not worthy to be there, that they aren't "spiritual"
enough or that they've done so many terrible things that
there is no way God could forgive them.

This reality has provided the answer to a question I've
often asked: Why is it that so many people can't get past
themselves and really enter into worship? It isn't that they
are afraid to sing, or they dislike the particular type of music

being played or sung. The problem is that *they don't feel welcome in God's presence*. They lack an understanding of the depth and gravity of God's love for them. They find it difficult to be in the presence of the One they have sinned against—they want to run and hide from Him, even though they have been forgiven.

There have been many times over the years that I have sensed God reaching down, taking a person's face in both of His hands, and looking that person in the eyes to say, "My son, My daughter, look at me. It's all right. I love you." Sadly, many don't respond to His loving invitation because they just can't convince themselves that they are welcome.

We in the Church often use another word for this feeling. Rather than say we don't feel "welcome," we say we don't feel "worthy." I struggle with that description because there are so many who really don't understand what the word "worthy" means. Believers often don't understand that their worthiness comes from Jesus—from His sacrifice for them.

In addition to feeling unworthy, perhaps fear is the stronghold that holds believers back. They are unsure of what's on the other side of the presence of God, and so they hold back, never fully surrendering to God. A stronghold for others may be rejection that causes them to retreat from any vulnerable position that could give opportunity to be rejected again.

David reminds us in Psalm 71:3 that God is *always* a fortress of safety to which we can go: "Be to me a protecting rock of safety, where I am always welcome" (*NLT*).

Here we see David running for his life from someone he loved very much—King Saul. Jonathon, Saul's son, whom David loved like a brother, was gone from David's life. David was now alone, suffering a terrible rejection; and yet he knew that God had never rejected him.

Maybe someone in your life fits this description. Maybe *you* fit this description. You may have endured heartache, and now you feel alone, rejected and exhausted from life's difficulties. Maybe life has not gone as you had planned, and you're living out the results of someone else's decisions. If that sounds like you, then remember the words of David: "Be to me a protecting rock of safety, where I am always welcome." Run into the circle of God's arms and know with all assurance that you are welcome there. God will never turn from you or close the door on you. His love is long-suffering and unconditional.

Romans 8:1 says, "Therefore, there is now *no* condemnation for those who are in Christ Jesus" (emphasis added). If that statement is true—and it is—then we must let go of the shame that keeps us from God. The truth of God's love is hard to receive when we hold on to the lie that we are not welcome; when we see forgiveness and restoration as a great party to which we are not invited; when we say things like, "Not me. I've done too much wrong in my life," or "If I share what's happened in my life, people will treat me differently." We need to reject the lie and receive the invitation to the celebration! God wants us to be with Him, completely restored and set free!

You are always welcome with God, so enter in and take your rightful place.

Sacred Expression

1. What instances in your life help you to relate to what five-year-old Jenna felt as she tried to adjust to yet another seemingly tenuous relationship in her life?

2. What about the nature of God brings out the wonder in your worship?

3. Consider times of personal worship when you have felt the wonder of God in your worship—and times when you have felt the absolute lack of it. What do you think could be the reasons for such a disparity of feelings during worship?

4. How should you respond when the King's eyes rest upon you?

5. Have you ever hidden your face from God? Why?

6. How can you keep shame from stealing the affectionate embrace God has for you?

7. Describe some of the times and situations in which you have felt unwelcome.

8. How has God personally ministered to you in those times?

The Divine Exchange

His Request: To accept what He's done
Our Reward: To be accepted

- When you choose to *reject* yourself out of shame, you are prioritizing your opinion over that of your Creator God.
- The beloved one in the Song of Songs assumed that the *king* was staring at her because he was judging her darkness.
- She responded defensively out of *shame* from the *exposure* of her life.
- The king described her beauty and *accepted* her despite the opinion of *others*.
- The king offered his beloved *security*.
- The King of kings *died* to provide us with unconditional love, acceptance and security.
- He made the *investment*.
- We must *accept* it.

Meet a Modern-Day Woman of Worship

Da'dra Crawford-Greathouse: "Acceptable"

If someone were to ask Da'dra how she became "anointed," she would admit that she is as puzzled as anyone by the path God has chosen for her life. Although she is now one-half of the group known as Anointed, she and her brother Steven—the other half of the group—could never have dreamed they would one day stand before thousands and sing.

In fact, when Da'dra was a child, there was no time for dreaming. It was hard enough for her to stand in front of her father and practice with her brother each Friday night. For more than four hours at a time, Da'dra and her brother would learn, sing and rehearse in hopes of reaching their father's standard of perfection.

Singing perfectly was Da'dra's dream, but not so that she could stand in front of cheering crowds. She sang with all her heart for the small chance that she might receive her father's approval. Her father held high musical standards for his children, particularly for Da'dra, but it seemed that no matter how hard she tried, her singing was never good enough. When she fell short of her father's expectations, he would lash out at her to the point of throwing the microphone and yelling his disapproval. Her mother would intervene, and her brother would stand in shock at the abusive demonstration aimed toward Da'dra.

But singing wasn't the only area in which Da'dra longed for unconditional acceptance. Her weight was also a constant point of contention with her father. Like any other little girl, she wanted to feel beautiful and be loved and protected as a precious daughter. But her father wanted physical perfection from her as well. The harder Da'dra tried to please him, the more she felt like a failure—and an ugly one at that.

The enemy was at work in all of this, trying to set a trap for her by creating an identity of unworthiness. The lie that he was speaking in her ear was something like this: "If your singing doesn't make you worthy, you have no talent, and if your appearance doesn't make you worthy of love, you must not have beauty worthy of protection."

To reinforce this filthy lie, the enemy staged a plan in the hope that Da'dra would truly believe she was worth nothing. One afternoon when she was about 15 years old, she waited at home after school for her mother to return from work. She had strict instructions not to let anyone in the house, and she had readily complied, as this rule made her feel safe as well as secure. But on this particular day, a young man she had known since she was very young knocked on the door and asked if she would sharpen some of his pencils—this wasn't a strange request because everyone knew her father had installed an industrial strength sharpener in the basement. When neighbors and friends wanted their pencils sharpened, they came knocking at Da'dra's door.

As Da'dra took the pencils and instructed the boy to wait outside, she shut the door and descended the stairs to the sharpener, although she never thought to lock the door, as this young man had been her friend for many years. As she rounded the corner back up the staircase, she ran into the boy, who had apparently followed her in. He threw her to the ground, struck her across the face and attempted to rape her. She couldn't believe he was serious, but the burning pain of her lip where he had hit her told her otherwise. She somehow managed to escape and ran upstairs, where he again trapped her, trying the same thing all over again.

Da'dra remembers calling out to God, asking Him to give her the strength to get free. In response, she felt a deep strength rising from within her, and she shoved the boy backward. He hit his head on a table. Fearing for her life, Da'dra ran to the kitchen and grabbed the largest knife she could find, and then she turned in his direction just as he was coming toward her. In that moment she spoke in her own defense, and her words cut him, though her knife did not. He left her house and her life without another word.

With the compounded message of unworthiness she felt from her father and then from this destructive, misguided young man, Da'dra searched for a place of complete acceptance. She began to sing privately in worship and to read her Bible regularly as a means of escape from everyday life. As she continued to create her own atmosphere of worship and relationship with God, a new and stronger message began to emerge. It was as if every time she sang, prayed and read her Bible, the voice of unworthiness and rejection was turned down, while the voice of unconditional love and acceptance was elevated in her ears.

And while this transformation did not happen overnight, it did happen. As she released the lie of the enemy, she was free to embrace the opinion of the King. Over time her true identity was found in the presence of the Most High God, and her confidence was restored.

"Vulnerable"

Surly you desire truth in the inner parts, you teach
me wisdom in the inmost place.

PSALM 51:6, *NIV*

Sarah had been in love with Ethan for as long as she could remember. But for just as long, she had known it was hopeless. Ethan was out of her league. He could have any woman he wanted, and there was no chance she would be the one he chose.

And so she said nothing.

She said nothing even when Ethan began to date Sarah's sister, Lynn, with whom she shared an apartment; even when Sarah knew that Lynn didn't really care about Ethan the way she did; even when Ethan's National Guard unit was called up for deployment to Iraq.

With tears in her eyes, Sarah watched Lynn scan Ethan's letters and then toss them aside as she ran out the door to

meet her friends. It wasn't until he came home on leave—
unannounced and unexpected—to find Sarah at home and
Lynn gone that Sarah knew she was finally going to have
to say something.

Hesitantly, she asked Ethan if he would like to take
a walk with her to the park. He agreed, and as they
walked, she told him that Lynn wasn't just out with her
friends—she was out with her new boyfriend. Everyone
in town knew about them, and Sarah thought it would
be kinder if she told Ethan rather than have him find
out from someone else, or worse yet, to see Lynn and her
boyfriend together.

Ethan took the news better than Sarah had expected.
In fact, he told her he had long suspected that Lynn was
seeing someone else, but when he had asked her about it,
she always changed the subject.

And then he told Sarah something that really shocked
her. He said that though he liked Lynn and had enjoyed
her company, it was really Sarah he had been attracted to
from the beginning. Yet she had seemed so quiet and
unapproachable that he had never had the nerve to ask
her for a date.

Imagine the surprise they shared when they discovered their long-standing mutual interest in one another—

not to mention their shared reluctance to be vulnerable and risk rejection. Their fear of vulnerability had nearly sabotaged what eventually turned out to be a very happy and successful marriage.

Fear of vulnerability is more common than most people realize, and that fear has sabotaged, prevented and destroyed countless relationships through the ages, simply because we are unwilling to be vulnerable and acknowledge *the truth of our lives*.

When Jesus spoke with the woman at the well, there came a turning point in the conversation when she had to acknowledge the truth of her life.

> He told her, "Go, call your husband and come back." "I have no husband," she replied. Jesus said to her, "You are right when you say you have no husband. The fact is, you have had five husbands, and the man you now have is not your husband. What you have just said is quite true" (John 4:16-18).

Jesus acknowledged that the woman had not lied to Him about her situation, though she had not spoken the whole truth. In the same way that God requires us to go deeper and to acknowledge the "loin cloth," or self-made covering, we use to hide our sin, Jesus zeroed in on what the woman at the well was hiding from Him. He obviously already knew everything about this woman, so why would He ask her about her life? And if He already knows all of our secrets—which, of course, He does—then why is it important for us to acknowledge hidden things?

It is for our own protection, not our embarrassment, that God tests our capacity for truth. He wants us to live in freedom, and revealing ourselves through vulnerability disarms our enemy. We have an enemy who uses our secrets as a weapon against us, who leads us to believe that we must keep parts of our life hidden. If we allow him to convince us that we cannot trust God with the revelation of who we really are, then our enemy holds the key to our secret place—and whoever holds the key also carries the authority. If we allow secret places for the enemy to dwell, we are essentially becoming more intimate with our enemy than with our Lord. This gives Satan power to destroy us from the inside out. If we cannot acknowledge the existence of such a place by seeking out our Savior and making ourselves vulnerable to Him, then we are not proving our willingness to hand over to Him the key to our heart.

In the Place of Truth

After Jesus spoke to the woman at the well about her private life, she sensed that He was a prophet, so she quickly changed the subject from her truth to her worship. The woman said to Him, "Sir, I perceive that You are a prophet. Our fathers worshiped on this mountain, and you Jews say that in Jerusalem is the place where one ought to worship" (John 4:19-20, *NKJV*).

Bless her heart; she had no idea that these two elements are intimately related. Jesus went on to explain to her, and now to us, that worship is a place of truth.

Jesus said to her, "Woman, believe Me, the hour is coming when you will neither on this mountain, nor in Jerusalem, worship the Father. You worship what you do not know; we know what we worship, for salvation is of the Jews. But the hour is coming, and now is, when the true worshipers will worship the Father in spirit and truth; for the Father is seeking such to worship Him. God is Spirit, and those who worship Him must worship in spirit and truth" (John 4:21-24, *NKJV*).

The woman obviously knew the history and methodology of worship, but Jesus made it clear that such things would soon have no bearing on true worship—or true worshipers. He also revealed to her the significance of the spiritual location where Jews and Samaritans would one day be united in worship. Because God is Spirit, He is not limited by the meeting places of man. He issues an open invitation to all who would pursue Him in spirit and truth. Jesus gave the woman directions to this place of worship that could not previously have been reached in her natural surroundings. There is a place to worship, Jesus explained, but it is not found on any map. The place of spirit and truth can only be found in the geography of the heart.

Truth is not easily stumbled upon. When everything in our nature tells us to protect ourselves and build walls around our heart, we may resist following the directions to the place of worship if it means that we must allow truth to lead us there. As we have witnessed in the story of the woman at the well, spending time with Jesus requires the truth, whether it comes about through confrontation or through vulnerability. Although God requires truth in worship, He does not force us to be vulnerable with Him. Vulnerability is an extended form of truth. It is an authentic, lavish initiative toward intimacy, an unmistakable overture.

When we set out on a quest for complete openness in our relationship with God—when being intimately known by God becomes a longing that we can no longer ignore—we are at a turning point on our journey of worship. If we want to experience more of God, we must first become willing to reveal more of ourselves.

It is no rare thing to know the identity of a celebrity. People are obsessed with reading about the lives of celebrities and sharing juicy bits of gossip about them with others. If I were one of those who "knew" certain celebrities in this way, I would really be only one of the millions who are familiar with the intimate details of these celebrities' lives. But for all of the knowledge that I might possess about these famous people, whether real or fabricated, it would draw me no closer to them. What does change the nature of the relationship is for the celebrities to know me. The power for intimacy is not in my knowledge of them but in their reciprocal knowledge of me.

The same is true of our relationship with God. Millions claim to know His nature. They call Him by name and discuss His ways. However, if we truly want an intimate relationship with God, we must seek Him out and make ourselves known to Him.

Worship Restores Intimacy

MARY ALESSI

I was born into a family that loved God and lived by faith every day. My parents were evangelists, and ours was a life lived on the road. My sisters and I sang along with our parents, and we had the privilege at very early ages to travel around the nation and sing together. What an exciting life for us girls! It was my great joy to lead people into the presence of God with singing. At the age of nine, I knew that music ministry was my calling in life.

I also knew a devastating secret shared only by the young girls in my family. Through a close relative, the enemy was stealing something priceless from us: our innocence. When we were between the ages of 8 and 13, this relative sought to molest my sisters and me, as well as our cousins. Sometimes he was successful, and sometimes he was not. My sisters and I had the fewest encounters with him, but we were still left to deal with this awful family secret.

Now, as an adult, I would be hard-pressed to remember all those terrible things that transpired during my childhood because God has truly healed and restored my heart and mind. I realize now what the enemy was truly after and what he worked to get from us through the abuse—our capacity for intimacy! You see, it takes an ability to be intimate, to feel comfortable with intimacy, in order to go deep with another person, let alone go deep with God Almighty. The devil may have fought to take us out, but God had already won the battle for us. What Satan meant for destruction and harm, God has turned around for our good. So much revelation has come out of that period of my life that I can't begin to tell you all He has done through it. I am a living testimony of the healing power of God.

If you enter God's presence withholding nothing, there is nothing He won't do to make you whole. When you are willing to become intimate with God, you give Him permission to heal the private wounds of your heart. And after private restoration comes public proclamation of His power and majesty!

Have You Seen My Lover?

Returning to our story of the shepherd-king and his beloved, we find in chapter 3 of the Song of Songs that the young woman is seeking the one she loves.

All night long on my bed I looked for the one my heart loves; I looked for him but did not find him (v. 1).

The beloved longed for her lover's presence in a way and in a place where she had not been with him before. She demonstrated a desire for something she had never had or experienced before. And in a dark and inconvenient time, she left her place of comfort to go and find him.

It is also in our darkest hours that we long for a closeness and intimacy that we have not yet experienced with God. The only solution is to get up and pursue Him with persistence.

> I will get up now and go about the city, through
> its streets ands squares; I will search for the one
> my heart loves. So I looked for him but did not
> find him. The watchmen found me as they made
> their rounds in the city. "Have you seen the one
> my heart loves?" Scarcely had I passed them when
> I found the one my heart loves. I held him and
> would not let him go till I had brought him to my
> mother's house, to the room of the one who con-
> ceived me (3:2-4).

She sought her lover with the intention of making herself vulnerable to him. When she found him, she would not let him go until she brought him "to the room of the one who conceived [her]." The only purpose for the inclusion of such detail is to make an important point. The account could easily have read "to her home," but the room where her mother conceived her would have been a very intimate place, and so the wording is quite deliberate. It was not a room for entertaining guests or for bringing strangers. Further, the beloved does not describe the room simply as a "conception" room, but shares her personal connection to it—the room was the place of *her* beginning, in *her* house, where *her* mother and father *conceived her.*

Her meaning is obvious in her use of descriptive words: By revealing this to him, she would have symbolically uncovered her life, showing him that nothing was hidden from him. She was giving him access to complete knowledge of her from the first moment of her existence, thereafter making every moment of her life accessible.

I Open My Heart

Now let's look at the lover's reaction to all this.

> You are a garden locked up, my sister, my bride;
> you are a spring enclosed, a sealed fountain (4:12).

After the lover has seen everything behind the "lock," he describes what he loves about his beloved in intimate terms. Although she has not yet given herself to him in a physical way, she has opened the door to intimacy by revealing to him all there is to know about herself. Once she has experienced this intimate encounter with him, she is set apart in her relationship with him. Even in a public place, the two of them carry on exchanges of intimacy because of what they have previously shared. This private experience spills over into open public affection.

It is the same with us: When we have taken our King into the secret places of our heart, we have reason to publicly celebrate His love and acceptance of us. For once we have encountered God, the Lover of our soul, we cannot remain unaffected or unmoved by His presence—publicly or privately.

On the subject of worship, my father has been quoted as saying, "If your worship doesn't move you, it probably won't move God." Based on the necessity for a reciprocal relationship in worship, it is apparent that God's response would be limited by our response to Him. God cannot accept what has not been given.

Worship is like dancing with the most graceful Partner. He takes a step toward me; I take a step closer to Him. Back and forth we go, giving and taking, with many exchanges that lead to a rhythm of relationship. We don't fear overstepping our bounds in this relationship, for God responds to every effort we make to come in sync with His heartbeat. Our overtures are not random acts, but they are all the more revealing and intimate as we draw nearer to Him.

Preparing for Intimacy

In our story, after the beloved has taken her step toward her lover by pursuing him, it is then her turn to be pursued. In the following text, she describes what she hears and feels in response to his arrival at her door.

> I slept but my heart was awake. Listen! My lover is knocking: "Open to me, my sister, my darling, my dove, my flawless one. My head is drenched with dew, my hair with the dampness of the night."
>
> I have taken off my robe—must I put it on again? I have washed my feet—must I soil them again?
>
> My lover thrust his hand through the latch-opening; my heart began to pound for him.
>
> I arose to open for my lover, and my hands dripped with myrrh, my fingers with flowing myrrh, on the handles of the lock.
>
> I opened for my lover, but my lover had left; he was gone. My heart sank at his departure (5:2-6).

How disappointing for her to be prepared and yet still unavailable. And how sad for him to seek her out and not be welcomed in response! So what can we learn from such an unfortunate scenario?

The text describes two reasons for her delay in welcoming him at the door. First, she was tired—she was asleep when he came knocking and calling for her. According to the previous verses, she had been preparing herself as a bride for her bridegroom. She had dressed in finery and covered herself with perfumed oil—and then she fell asleep. With all that preparation, we know she must have deeply desired to be perfectly ready for his arrival, and yet her weariness overwhelmed her eager heart.

Although her heart wanted to run to him, her flesh found it too inconvenient, and her tiredness made her susceptible to the will of the flesh. She had spent all of her energy making herself beautiful and fragrant on the outside, but she had not prepared her heart to respond properly when the moment of his arrival came. She wasn't prepared for the inevitable battle between her spirit and her flesh. As a result, her flesh held her back, though her spirit wanted to respond.

Jesus pointed out this universal problem quite clearly in Matthew 26:41, when He warned, "Watch and pray, lest you enter into temptation. The spirit indeed is willing, but the flesh is weak" (*NKJV*). All of the preparation that made the beloved so weary had been measured out upon herself, leaving nothing in the way of energy or affection for her lover. Apparently she forgot that the purpose behind the preparation was for his pleasure, not her own. Maybe if she had put more thought into the relationship beyond the courtship, she might have saved something for later.

In fact, the beloved's outward preparation is the second stumbling block for the doomed encounter with intimacy. Once she realized what she had done, she rushed to the door, but the oil on her hands caused her to fumble and further delay the opening. It seems that she went a bit overboard with the preparations. To have oil literally dripping down her fingertips tells us that she put on a little too much, to say the least.

The beloved's delayed response to her lover's call ultimately cost her the intimate encounter she had so longed to experience. But what were the real reasons for her missed opportunity? Was it simply because she was tired and oily, or is there an important connection between these two factors that tell us where the true path to disappointment began for her? Let me propose that she was both tired and abundantly covered with oil for the same reason. She had spent all of her time and attention preparing the outside appearance, while completely ignoring the need to cultivate and prepare the internal response of her spirit.

Preparing herself outwardly didn't conflict with the flesh because the process was pleasing, agreeable and self-affirming. But preparing the internal environment for intimacy is an entirely different story. It is not quite so simple, because it doesn't soothe and make us feel good the way external indulgences often do.

So what could the beloved have done to properly prepare her heart to meet her lover?

Evidence that the internal environment has been prepared is that there is an overabundance of willingness to endure the inconvenient for the remote chance of expressing the essence of sacrificial love. Oil, which is the symbol of sacrifice, is applied externally to prepare the outside, but the real essence of sacrificial love must be expressed internally if the outside beautification is to have any meaning. In the case of the beloved, when it came down to choosing sacrificial love by moving beyond the comfortable, she could not manage the right decision. She loved preparing herself when it was all about her, but the moment she had to choose between her comfort and her lover, she hesitated.

He was outside her door and clearly willing to endure the dampness of the night to find her, but he was met with hesitation instead of anticipation. It was her hesitation that made her preparation pointless. By the time she finally opened the door, the one she had wanted to see was gone. She had chosen the synthetic symbols of sacrifice over the authentic essence of complete vulnerability.

How many times have we applied the oil of anointing, thinking all the while that it is for our pleasure when it is really supposed to be applied in preparation for Him? Have we misunderstood the purpose for anointing in our lives? Where would God prefer that we spend our time preparing?

I am sure that the lover would have preferred to find his beloved ready, waiting and available—but she wasn't. And even though he had previously been behind the locked door, he did not have the key.

> Here I am! I stand at the door and knock. If any-
> one hears my voice and opens the door, I will come
> in and eat with [her], and [she] with me (Rev. 3:20).

Eventually the beloved did find her lover in the night, but she had to go out and search for him. It is the same in our relationship with Jesus. When we seek Him, He is there for us. When we long for Him and call on Him, He comes to us. In fact, Jesus has already come to us. He now stands at the door, waiting for us to wake up and let Him in.

When He seeks you, will you be found prepared—ready and waiting? Or will you be sleeping behind a locked door, hesitating to let Him in because your spirit is unprepared?

Vulnerability is the willingness and the ability to make ourselves totally and completely available. This is the only way to conceive the heart and will of God in our lives—by making ourselves completely vulnerable. Because of God's unwillingness to push Himself upon us, we must take the responsibility to make ourselves available. God has already done all that He can to pave the way for intimate relationship with us. He is a Gentleman and a servant of the highest esteem. He did not put on flesh in an "act" of servanthood; that is who He is. He is a Servant, a Savior, a Shepherd . . . and a King.

Sacred Expression

1. When have you, like Sarah or Ethan, missed an opportunity to relate to someone on a deeper level because you were afraid to be vulnerable?

2. When have you lied—or at least covered or softened the truth—in an effort to make others think more highly of you? What were the results?

3. Why does God require us to acknowledge the "loin cloth" we use to cover ourselves?

4. Have you ever felt as if your "secret places" have given the enemy access to your life?

5. How did you feel when you first realized that God had accepted you just as you are?

6. Knowing now that God has already accepted you, in what new way will you let Him in?

7. What can you do to help ensure that you won't slip back into the old ways of trying to "cover" yourself?

8. What process of preparation have you undergone to make yourself ready for a deeper relationship with God?

The Divine Exchange

His Request: To reveal ourselves
Our Reward: To receive revelation

• Beloved *revealed* herself to him.
• He came to *visit* her unannounced.

- She was weary with *preparation*.
- She *missed* her moment.
- Her application of *anointing oil* had been overwhelmingly spent on herself at the expense of her bridegroom.
- Being *available* to Him is just as valuable as being *vulnerable* with Him.
- When I *reveal myself* to God, He will *reveal Himself* to me—this is the divine exchange available through intimate worship.

Meet a Modern-Day Woman of Worship
Martha Munizi: "Vulnerable"

Although Martha Munizi is known for her soulful sound-track "Glorious" and her upbeat, encouraging style of leading worship, her life has not always been so glorious. To look at her you would think she had never had a bad day. Martha is blonde, beautiful, talented and anointed. But she would readily say that her darkest days were the ones that most punctuated her calling. There is no shortage of gifted, anointed people who want to be used by God to lead others in worship, but there is definitely a lack of attention given to the process that purifies one's calling.

The attack against Martha's unstoppable anointing started when she was just a baby. The enemy had plans to eliminate her at a young age, and she almost died from spinal meningitis. Doctors gave her parents no hope for her life and no options for treatment. But God miraculously touched her body, healed her and took all the credit. Martha knows that her life is not her own, and she now lives to lift up the name of Jesus. But Martha's testimony doesn't just encourage us regarding physical healing, for she has been touched by emotional healing as well.

When Martha was a teenager, her world was shaken by the sudden divorce of her parents. She had known a certain amount of celebrity due to the renowned musical career of her father. And her mother had loved, supported and sacrificed much of her own life to make her husband's and children's dreams come true. So it was only natural during Martha's experience of the divorce and subsequent feelings of abandonment that she question God's perfect plan. The turmoil and tragedy of Martha's broken home caused her to reevaluate the foundation upon which her faith was built. Did her sole identity spring from her parents? How would she respond to the questions and opinions of others? Did the unfortunate outcome of her parents' relationship change the way she would go about trusting her husband and other spiritual leaders?

Question by question, she had to address and dismiss the voice of the enemy and choose again to make herself vulnerable to the calling God had upon her life. She knew that to internalize her disappointment in life would leave her vulnerable to the enemy. And if the devil could cause her to harbor unanswered questions about the faithfulness of God, Martha would never rise to fully trust God again.

Martha chose not to listen to the enemy but to focus instead on the greatness and faithfulness of God. Her vow shines through every lyric Martha writes or sings. Those who hear her voice are blessed by her living testimony.

"Broken"

Be imitators of God, therefore, as dearly loved children and
live a life of love, just as Christ loved us and gave himself up
for us as a fragrant offering and sacrifice to God.

EPHESIANS 5:1-2

Author Patsy Clairmont has written a wonderful book titled *God Uses Cracked Pots*—and she is absolutely right! Though she approaches the subject with a touch of humor, she is stating a very powerful principle of God's kingdom: Before God can effectively use us, He must break through all of our outer layers of self-protective armor so that the fragrance of His love and mercy can "leak" out onto others.

One of the mysteries of the Kingdom is the fact that to be whole we must first become broken. There are several logical reasons for this that can be understood, in part, by the mind of the flesh. However, for the most part, it is only in the spirit that we can fully comprehend this concept. To become broken means that internal meets external, as in the moment when a flower reaches its most fragrant point and is then crushed, releasing the sweet smelling oil. If the flower were to fade and die, it would lose the potency of its aroma. But when the essence is released at the right time, the moment is preserved forever in the fragrant oil.

During the process of writing this book, I came across a magazine interview with a famous perfumer who had been hired to formulate designer fragrances. As he described the process of extracting oils for perfume, I couldn't help but see a strong similarity between his thoughts on fragrance and my thoughts on worship. This man felt that bottling perfume was an act of truth because of its simplicity. He would withdraw the essence from the flower or herb and then let the scent speak for itself. The complicated part of his job was the act of re-creating the illusion of truth for the inexpensive alcohol-based version of the same fragrance. Without using any oils from the original flowers, he had to layer synthetic scents to create an illusion that would ultimately smell much like the original, expensive perfume made from oils.

Good-Bye to Me

The perfume-making process is very much like worship. We can create truth by sacrificing the external for the sake of the internal. Granted, it is extremely expensive, as it may cost us all we have. Then again, we may choose a much cheaper alternative, which is to layer synthetic symbols of the truth by creating our own "perfume." We may put on a good act of dying to self and sacrificing our agendas and desires, but in the end we're offering substitutes for the real thing. Both versions will smell similar in the beginning, but only the real thing will linger and last. Most important, God knows the difference. Nothing can compare to the fragrant aroma of real sacrifice, and anyone who has experienced it would never count the cost.

Old Testament Worship and Sacrifice

In Old Testament times, worship and sacrifice were synonymous. When Abraham said, "I will go to the mountain to worship," he did not mean that he would climb to the top and then dance, sing and play a tambourine. Noah, Abraham and Moses all knew that worship requires a sacrificial offering that sends an aroma heavenward. The offering of worship was not just a demonstrative act performed in an effort to please God. Rather, it was a meaningful, costly experience for the one making the offering. The animals that were chosen for sacrifice held a high value in the lives of the people of the Old Testament. So when an animal was given as an act of worship, it was a true sacrifice on the part of those who were making the offering.

The other important factor involved in Old Testament worship and sacrifice was the role of the animal, who took the place of the one making the offering. The worshiper would place his hand upon the head of the animal in a symbolic gesture that said, "This is me." So, in effect, the animal stood in as a substitute for the one making the offering and died in his or her place. Because Jesus died as the ultimate, once-for-all sacrifice for our sin, we no longer have to sacrifice animals to cover our sins and obtain God's forgiveness (see Heb. 10:1-18).

The Old Testament sacrifices were not only sin offerings. By sacrificing animals, the Israelites maintained their relationship with God. When the Israelites were willing to offer God valuable sacrifices, He knew they really wanted His presence in their lives because it cost them something. After Jesus fulfilled the Law by becoming the supreme blood sacrifice, we experienced true and everlasting atonement and were brought into a living covenant with God.

Jesus' Sacrifice and Our Worship

In response to all these marvelous things, hear what Paul says: "I appeal to you therefore, brothers and sisters, by the mercies of God, to present your bodies as a living sacrifice, holy and acceptable to God, which is your spiritual worship" (Rom. 12:1, *NRSV*). In different language, but getting at the same idea, Jesus said, "If any of you wants to be my follower you must put aside your selfish ambition, shoulder your cross, and follow me. If you try to keep your life for yourself, you will lose it. But if you give up your life for my sake and for the sake of the Good News, you will find true life" (Mark 8:34-35, *NLT*). These passages show that worship and sacrifice are two ideas that you just can't separate. Even though salvation is free—"by grace through faith" (Eph. 2:8-9)—if you want to worship, it's going to cost something. There's no getting around it. In giving our all in worship, we are united with Jesus not only through His death but through our own as well.

After all, how can we relate to Jesus' sacrifice if we are unwilling to lay down our own lives? We must place our hand upon those things that give us the most value and say, "This represents me—all of me." Then, leading those things to the altar, we say good-bye. It is only in giving Him the things that bring us our value that we can truly take on the nature of worship and be called "a living sacrifice." Giving Him all that we have says, at least in some small way, that we long to acquaint ourselves with His sacrifice.

Sacrificial Love

We have looked at the love affair between the beloved and her lover in the Song of Songs—how she worshiped in wonder, covered her face in shame, accepted his approval, showed him her secrets and then missed her moment for intimacy. Thankfully, that is not where the story ends. After she opened the door and found that she had waited too long and he was gone, she ventured out to capture him once again.

> I looked for him but did not find him. I called him but he did not answer.
> The watchmen found me as they made their rounds in the city. They beat me, they bruised me; they took away my cloak (5:6-7).

The description of her abuse rings with familiarity. As we know, Jesus was also mistreated in the same fashion. He was beaten, He was bruised, and they cast lots for His cloak. We know from being on the receiving end of the benefits of Christ's sacrifice on the cross that there is nothing like suffering to solidify a commitment to someone. To embrace the horrible manner in which Jesus died makes us all the more passionate for Him, because He suffered for us. Many of us have no idea how far we would go to save someone we love, and there is no test to try us but suffering. If we are willing and determined to love despite unfortunate encounters, we love sacrificially.

There is no given reason for the watchmen to have treated the beloved so bitterly. Yet from that point on, she begins to describe her lover in a profoundly different way. For the first time she recognizes what is so unique and special about him. The sacrifice she endured in search of him gave her clarity of purpose and an intimate connection to his unique identity that she didn't have before. She then knew him so well, in fact, that she immediately realized where to find him without searching aimlessly.

My lover has gone down to his garden, to the beds of spices, to browse in the gardens and to gather lilies.
   I am my lover's and my lover is mine; he browses among the lilies (6:2-3).

Building a Wall

There are no satisfactory reasons that can explain away the pain and torture of our lives. If we could hear the answer to why horrible things have happened to us, it still would not satisfy our pain and brokenness. The only salve is to see that the real purpose for our brokenness is to acquaint us with the sacrifice of Jesus. We can create altars of worship made from the stones of our experiences (stones are the broken pieces left over from the erosion and upheaval of the earth). When our life blows up in our face, we too are left with fragments of the existence we once knew.

Usually we make one of two choices when we encounter brokenness: We use the stones of our experience to build an altar or we use them to erect a wall. When we are devastated by circumstances that make us feel vulnerable, broken and exposed to pain, we are tempted to choose to survive by preserving what we can of the broken pieces. Knowing that we must do something with the heaviness in our lives, we begin to lug stones around, placing them around us for protection. This protection turns to fortification: Walls are erected, defenses set and flags fly with the words "I will never be broken again."

These walls make us feel safe and secure, but they also make it difficult, often impossible, to move forward. How can we stay in one spot to protect the past and yet move on into the future? It can't be done. When we choose to build a stronghold, we are no longer free to leave, because we have walled ourselves inside as the fierce defenders of our own personal fortress. We can never move beyond that point of devastation without dismantling the wall, lowering our defenses and going back to the place in time when it all began. By breaking down the walls we have worked so hard to build, we are then able to choose again what to do with the stones of our experience.

Unlike building a wall, when we choose to build an altar with the stones of our experience, we are free to move on. After we have dedicated that portion of our lives to Him, we can celebrate the journey into the future.

Building a Memorial

We must remember that God does not require inconvenient things of us just to make our lives harder. What He is telling us is that the best time to "gather stones" from our experience is when we are right in the middle of them.

> "In the future, when your children ask you, 'What do these stones mean?' tell them that the flow of the Jordan was cut off before the ark of the covenant of the LORD. When it crossed the Jordan, the waters of the Jordan were cut off. These *stones* are to be a memorial to the people of Israel forever."
>
> So the Israelites did as Joshua commanded them. They took twelve stones from the middle of

the Jordan, according to the number of the tribes of the Israelites, as the LORD had told Joshua; and they carried them over with them to their camp, where they put them down. Joshua set up the twelve stones that had been in the middle of the Jordan at the spot where the priests who carried the ark of the covenant had stood. And they are there to this day (Josh. 4:6-9, emphasis added).

To stop in the center of the journey and retrieve every rock of understanding and carry them out of the experience is the most honorable way to memorialize God's hand in our deliverance. He is a God worthy of memorial when we are right in the middle of a painful circumstance, struggling to hold up all that He represents in our lives.

In Memory of Her . . .

I tell you the truth, wherever the gospel is preached throughout the world, what she has done will also be told, in memory [memorial] of her.
Mark 14:9

The primary use for the word "memorial" in our modern culture is centered on death. We don't typically memorialize something that is still alive; neither does God. Memorials are rarely mentioned in Scripture without the inclusion of stones, sacrifice or scent. Each of these elements represents something dead or broken, and yet has the power to draw the attention of God and men.

> Then Mary took about a pint of pure nard, an expensive perfume; she poured it on Jesus' feet and wiped his feet with her hair. And the house was filled with the fragrance of the perfume (John 12:3).

Breaking the Box

She broke the jar [box] and poured the
perfume on his head.
Mark 14:3

By breaking the box and releasing its costly contents upon the feet of Jesus, Mary turned her past experiences into worship. Although we do not know how or where she got the expensive perfume, we do know that it was either a gift from someone in her past or that she had used money previously earned to purchase the box. Either way, Mary's alabaster box represented her past, her memories, her experiences and her reputation. The pain of our past is one of the most expensive and valuable gifts we can give to God because it is all we have in the present. Worship is a way of gift-wrapping our pain and our past into the present and then giving them over to God.

Mary's box also represented the future. The alabaster box, in her time, was often given by the bride as a dowry for marriage in recognition of transferring the woman's wealth to her husband. This knowledge sheds further light on Mary's sacrifice. Mary was giving to Jesus her only chance for marriage and financial security. Whatever hopes rested on or within that box were broken by her hands. By giving Jesus her future hope, she was declaring that one moment with Him was more precious to her than a lifetime with anyone else.

We, not unlike Mary, have costly containers of our own. The boxes of our heart that keep us compartmentalized and incongruent can be broken through one act of extravagant worship. Brokenness equals wholeness when the walls of our heart are broken down, for only then can the essence of our anointing pour out upon the Body of Christ.

Teach me your way, O LORD, and *I will walk in your truth*; give me an undivided heart, that I may fear your name. I will praise you, O Lord my God, with all my heart; I will glorify your name forever (Ps. 86:11-12, emphasis added).

The Beauty of Brokenness

Honor God by building a memorial to the experiences He has brought you through. If you are reliving the painful response of devastation, then contemplate your proximity to a wall. You may be standing behind your own opportunity to choose brokenness by breaking down the boundary you have set around your heart. God will empower you to make a quick work of dismantling your defenses. Every heavy thing you set aside will only serve to make your path out of prison a smooth one. You don't have to understand why God allowed you to suffer pain in order to feel worthy to create a memorial. The only thing you need to know is that you will, in time, see the beauty of brokenness.

Without question, my most broken moment ultimately became my most beautiful memorial. As a young single woman, I had a perfect image of what I believed wholeness should look like. As a pastor's daughter, my perspective in life was formed from the perilous perch of judgment. I would see wonderful people get themselves into horrible situations and respond by thinking, *I guess I really didn't know them very well.* Through those formidable years, I removed myself from any situation that would have caused me to "fall from grace." I wanted to be a spotless, perfect bride when I married, and I chose remote living as a protective path for my life. Because I was not personally acquainted with brokenness, I thought personal purity was found in perfection.

All the while my heart cried out to be used by God to minister healing to those who needed the comfort of the Holy Spirit. But I had no grace to give. I tried to label everything either black or white because of my belief that if I could control my behavior, then others should be able to completely avoid temptation as well. And if they couldn't remain pure, then in my mind they were simply no longer qualified to minister to others. What I had failed to understand was that even the sweetest newborn is not pure—the Bible says that we are all born into sin.

My pride played out just the way the Word of God says it will—with a fall. I met Stacey, the man of my dreams, and I fell twice. I fell in love and I fell from my high horse. I fell not from grace but into the arms of it.

After becoming engaged and discussing our winter wedding, Stacey and I found our familiarity went too far beyond planning. Since I was sure that he was the man for me, I felt no reservations and saw no red flags, as I had in previous relationships. Although keeping myself pure for marriage was the right thing to do, my motivation to do so was solely out of pride. And eventually I took the dive with no parachute.

Stacey and I were both regretful and repentant for overstepping the boundaries of our engagement. We knew that we had created a much more difficult beginning for ourselves by sleeping together before we were married. Immediately a sense of jealousy and suspicion, which had not been a part of our lives or our relationship, began to nag at us, causing us to question one another. I suppose it came from the disturbing thought that if we could not trust ourselves together, how could we trust ourselves or each other when we were apart?

We knew that we were right for each another, but we were sorry we had endangered our relationship by eating from forbidden fruit. So we promised one another that we would not cross the line again. Continuing to make our plans to be together, I went home at the end of my second year of college to prepare for my fiancé to move to Dallas as well.

Shortly after I returned home, I got really sick. After a rough week or so of what I thought was the flu, I realized that what I was dealing with was pregnancy. Although I had lost my perch of judgment a while back, my public dream of perfection was only now beginning to resemble a nightmare.

I had always wanted to get married and be a mother, and I was thrilled at the thought of that; but in spite of the positive aspects of the situation, I could only focus on the failure and disappointment. I feared that my situation would cast a shadow on my parents and somehow people would find a way to blame them for my choices—though my parents had never been anything but graciously real and transparent toward me. They did not deserve a selfish daughter who could have—and should have—waited a little longer. Then I thought about my call to ministry and how I was no longer qualified to serve. I assumed that everyone would say, "We thought Amie was a good girl. I guess we really didn't know her all that well!" And I just knew that I would be judged by anyone who heard the news of this poor pitiful pastor's daughter who had made a big mistake.

The reason I felt that my parents would disown me, my friends reject me and strangers talk about me was because, until that moment, that is exactly how I would have responded had I been in their shoes. I thank God that the ones whom I feared would judge, reject and slander me responded with the grace of God. Two days after I found out I was pregnant, I began to miscarry. I was well on my way to losing the baby, and no one else besides my parents even knew about the pregnancy. Instead of standing by waiting for the verdict, my parents prayed over me. Only grace could make a way for my parents to pray that my child would live and not die, that he would be born to fulfill his destiny on this earth. Knowing what they were about to face, my parents prayed for the will of God to be fulfilled through the life of my unborn child.

As ministers of God's Word, my parents were people of authentic integrity, yet I was still amazed at the way they embraced my brokenness and showed me a fountain of unlimited grace and mercy. I realized then that my mother and father must have known and experienced a side of God that I had never seen up close.

My parents, with utter transparency, guided Stacey and me through the difficult decisions we were facing. We all shared the feeling that telling our friends, family and church family was the only way to go. I was prepared for the harsh reception I fully expected to receive; but instead I found only grace and acceptance in the arms of the Body of Christ. The same people whom I had thought were disqualified through their own mistakes welcomed me into the brotherhood of brokenness.

This beautiful death of my dreams taught me something about life and the path I had been on. You see, I could not have led others on the path of restoration and healing had I not walked that road myself. The very thing that was meant to disqualify me actually accomplished just the opposite, for I had been far more unqualified without grace. Getting grace, the offspring of brokenness, was my greatest reward, a memorial I would never trade for an image of perfection.

In the beginning of this situation, I could not wrap my brain around why God, in His grace, would allow me to go through something so traumatic. Originally, all I could think of were the others I knew who, in my opinion, had gotten away with years of compromise with seemingly no consequences. So when I found myself in that situation, I had many questions for God, most of which began with "Why me?" It was only through the passage of time that I came to realize that His grace actually kept me from something far more tragic than an unplanned pregnancy. Through my failure, God turned up the soil in my life, revealing the stones of sin.

I now understand that purity is a process brought on by the brokenness of our lives. We are born with boulders of sin buried deep beneath the surface. Through upheaval we come to a place of making a choice. We can either use the boulders to build a wall to keep out pain or to build a memorial to the grace of God that heals our pain.

The public way in which this event happened to me was necessary for my heart and my behavior to become congruent, causing the internal motivation to be aligned with the external demonstration. God was doing me a favor by revealing a boulder in my life that would otherwise have made me fall again and again. Had I not had the wisdom of my parents to guide me, I probably would have hidden my mistake and begun a double life of outward judgment and inward shame.

So how did things eventually turn out? Stacey and I were married a few months earlier than planned, and we have been happily married ever since. We spent the first months of our marriage repairing the damage of lost trust, as anyone who crosses the line before they wed will tell you must be done. But we were committed to one another and to the belief that God knew what was best for both of us. When I look back to the most defining moment of my life, I see a fork in the road. I chose to take a dramatic turn away from the illusion of perfection toward the path to real purity—and it was the wisest choice I've ever made.

I believe that we are all defined not so much by our mistakes but by the decisions that follow them. If we choose repentance and run to God in worship, we receive the grace to change the course of our lives. The enemy inaccurately predicted my response to brokenness; for what was meant for evil, God turned to good. I not only received an endowment of grace, but I also received a son of grace, my sweet boy Grayson.

Each memorial will tell its own story of deliverance, leaving a marker of the grace of God for others to see and follow. My prayer for you is that you will one day embrace your "son of grace" as the blessing of brokenness it was meant to be. What a wonderful opportunity we have to gather all of the stones of our experiences and stack them up before the Lord, making our broken things the foundation for our worship—our altar.

> Therefore, I urge you, [sisters], in view of God's mercy, to offer your bodies as living sacrifices, holy and pleasing to God—this is your spiritual act of worship (Rom. 12:1).

I Worship You with All of Me

MARY ALESSI

When it comes to worship, there is no greater worshiper than the psalmist David, a man after God's own heart (see Acts 13:22). David sought to know God's heart, not just His will. So many of us seek only after God's will, desiring to know how He wants to use us, but David longed for the Person of God, to know Him in a deep way.

David's depth spilled over into his public worship. In 2 Samuel 6:14, David danced before the Lord with total abandon. He took his celebration to the streets as he worshiped his way back with the Ark of the Covenant. With him were all the people of Israel, celebrating and singing songs as they traveled. King David had a heart to celebrate God and was not about to hold back his passion. In a very public display of affection, David danced and sang openly, unadorned, as a common man. Imagine a king or a president dancing before the Lord openly, publicly, for the world to see!

King David loved God and was not embarrassed to show it. His dancing and singing may have cost him the affection of his wife Michal, but not the affection of God. God saw that David gave everything in worship. His private and public feelings for God were evident through His united expression of worship.

If only we could show such genuine affection in our worship! Believers are often challenged in their ability to

worship demonstratively or are limited in their inward communion with God. Many times we focus on one or the other: the external expression of our body or the internal position of our heart. David's worship shows us that both are equally important to God. It is vital that we be alone with Him and let Him search us and be known by Him in an intimate way. But it is also crucial that we have the ability to celebrate our relationship publicly.

We know that David did both of these things with regularity. In the psalms we read his private struggles in worship and intimate conversations with God, and it soothes us to know that we can go to God, bearing our soul, and be accepted by Him. God's heart, or desire, for us is to be whole. And when we give Him everything, all that we are, in worship, He is able to bring that wholeness and healing.

To worship Him with all of me means that there is no area of my life that worship cannot touch. And when worship flows from the inside out, I am made whole by the connection of internal and external worship becoming one flowing expression.

If you desire to know God in a deeper way, all you have to do is ask. Just pray, "Father God in heaven, I want more of You. I want my worship to be truthful, honest, uninhibited and full of passion for You." Ask Him for more of Himself, and don't stop asking until He fills you to overflowing! Just remember that when you give Him your all, He will give you His.

Sacred Expression

1. Whether or not you are familiar with Patsy Clairemont's book, can you think of at least one way your life relates to the concept that God uses cracked pots?

2. List some of your personal "crushing" experiences that have released the fragrance of God's love and mercy to flow out of you to others.

3. How did this vulnerability and brokenness make you feel about yourself and about God?

4. Have you gathered the stones of remembrance from these experiences? If not, what holds you back from doing so now?

5. How might you dedicate your personal memorials of worship?

6. How have the opinions of others held you back from submitting to God's crushing experience for your life?

7. Why do you think King David was able to worship God with such abandon, even to the point that his own wife looked on him with contempt?

8. What changes can you make in your own life to help you be more open to God's crushing so that you might carry His presence in your life?

The Divine Exchange

His Request: A sacrificial death
Our Reward: An aromatic life

- Throughout the Bible, memorials to God were made from *stones* and *scents*.
- Stones were symbols of strength through *brokenness*.
- Scents were symbolic of the *death* of an offering.
- When we encounter brokenness, we can choose to build a *wall* of defense or a *memorial* of worship.
- God's command to Joshua shows us that the most important time to gather our "stones" is when we are right in the *middle* of our trial.
- Mary of Bethany broke her alabaster jar on the feet of Jesus as a fragrant *offering*.
- The alabaster jar represented her past, *present* and future.

Meet a Modern-Day Woman of Worship

Cindy Cruse-Ratcliff: "Broken"

The world took notice when the megachurch of Lakewood in Houston, Texas, introduced their vibrant new worship leader, Cindy Cruse-Ratcliff, on their weekly television show. But Cindy is no stranger to a crowd. In fact, her renowned career as a Christian songwriter began at nine years of age when her first song was registered with ASCAP. From a very young age, Cindy's talent and anointing were evident and brought her great favor with God and man. She grew up touring with her father, mother, brothers and sisters as they sang and ministered together across the country. While traveling, she met and married a young man with singing talent of his own. Together Cindy and her husband wrote and produced many popular songs for well-known artists.

As time passed, Cindy grew more passionate than ever about serving God and the Body of Christ, but she found herself living much of her life alone. Her husband's success had brought a change in his focus, which in turn greatly affected their personal and work relationships. More and more she found herself going to great lengths to accommodate any opportunity to see her husband. Cindy slowly began to accept that spending time together was no longer a priority for him as it was for her. Despite her best efforts, it was becoming clear that he had made another life without her. But despite the rejection and pain she felt, Cindy would not leave her husband. She was determined to give God the opportunity to turn the situation around. She remained loyal until the door closed completely on the marriage.

It was at this stage in her life that Cindy came to Covenant Church in north Dallas where she served as a leading member of the worship team. Over the four years Cindy spent leading worship at Covenant Church, God continued to restore and prepare her for greater things.

In the year 1999, Cindy's friends and family were blessed to watch as God brought a wonderful, faithful man into her life. Marcus and Cindy were married in a sacred celebration that truly was a demonstration of the faithfulness of God to restore to us that which is greater than our loss. God has uniquely made her husband, Marcus, to love, support and empower Cindy to walk in her calling and anointing. It is as if all the loyalty she sowed into her first marriage has been returned to her, through the faithfulness of God, in the form of a wonderful prince. After Marcus and Cindy were married, Pastor Joel Osteen called from Lakewood in Houston, Texas, to offer her a job, and the newlyweds moved to the next level—together!

Although Cindy has made wise decisions throughout her life, the choices she made *during her season of brokenness* were what led her to the fairytale existence she now lives. So when you see Cindy worship and when you hear her sing, just remember that God sees the secret sacrifices and rewards them openly. He will do the same for you! If you will be faithful to God, you will reap the rewards of His faithfulness on your behalf.

"Overshadowed"

I sing in the shadow of your wings.

PSALM 63:7

Kerri was raised in an abusive home and spent the better part of her childhood watching her father use her mother as a punching bag. At the age of 15, Kerri ran away with Steve, a handsome but unemployed 25-year-old alcoholic who promised her a new life. Sadly, all she ended up with was a rerun of her old life, only this time she was the punching bag.

When her own daughter, Melissa, was born, Kerri determined not to expose her child to the same upbringing she'd had. She decided to run away again—this time to a shelter at a nearby church. While there Kerri gave her heart to the Lord, and at last found the new life she had been seeking. With the abuse behind her, she felt confident that she could raise her little girl in a safe, healthy, loving environment.

And then one Sunday morning, as she sat in church, the pastor began to teach on the biblical principle of the need for wives to submit to their husbands. Kerri was horrified. She wondered, *Had her mother been right in staying with her abusive husband? Had Kerri been wrong to flee her situation? Must a wife willingly put up with any treatment her husband chose to mete out?*

She was nearly ready to jump up and run out the back door when the pastor said something that grabbed her heart and convinced her to stay.

"One of the meanings of submission," he said, "is to come underneath in a safe place. That's why we can submit to God without fear, knowing that when we hide ourselves under the shadow of His wing, we are safe. If husbands and wives regularly understood and practiced that meaning of submission, there would be little need to preach about it from the pulpit, and there would be a lot more happy couples filling our pews every Sunday."

Kerri felt the tension go out of her shoulders and the joy return to her heart. She had come to the right place after all, the safe place where perfect love casts out all fear (see 1 John 4:18).

Under the shadow of God's protective wings . . .

Overshadowed by God's love and protection . . .

The use of the word "overshadowed" has taken on a meaning that has come to be regarded as negative. No one in our modern society wants to be overshadowed, especially women who, in more recent history, have seen and celebrated the outline of their own shadow upon society. So why would anyone choose to be in or under the shadow of something greater? That is a question posed by this modern world and answered by the Spirit of God. Only in the kingdom of heaven is the nature of over-shadowing truly all it was meant to be.

We can overlay the Kingdom of heaven upon our lives and let it show us the way to truth. The Kingdom's path is an *opposite* path from the way of the world. I often refer to the Kingdom as "upside down" because the Lord's value system is the exact opposite of the world's values. (I have since come to understand that this world is actu-ally the "upside down" kingdom, because God's king-dom is the true Kingdom.) Understanding the kingdom of God is all about receiving eternal perspective. When we come to ourselves in the mighty revelation that we were first born of the Kingdom through the heart of the Creator, our perspective of who we are spiritually will fundamentally renew our minds and our responses to this temporary life.

> Do not conform any longer to the pattern of this world, but be transformed by the renewing of your mind (Rom. 12:2).

Overshadowing—an intimate encounter with God—is experienced when our spirit is *willing, accepting, vulnerable, broken and available*. Like a combination lock that goes from one degree of openness to another until all are in proper alignment, so does worship take us through each relationship requirement until we stand completely open to the work of the Holy Spirit.

Available

The pattern of this world tells us to fight for our independent identity, while the Kingdom tells us that we have been designed for illumination only in the hands of our Creator. From magazine ads to television commercials, we are given the worldly pattern for beauty, to which we strive to conform. Yet in the Kingdom, our affirmation and beauty come to us as a result of the reflection of His glory. Even when Jesus went to the mountain to pray,

His countenance was changed by the glory of God. We now refer to the place of that experience as the Mount of Transfiguration.

> And as He prayed, the appearance of His face was altered, and His robe became white and glistening. Then behold, two men talked with Him, who were Moses and Elijah, who appeared in glory and spoke of His decease which He was about to accomplish at Jerusalem (Luke 9:29-31, *NKJV*).

The transformation Jesus underwent as a result of going to the mountain prepared Him to endure the temporary in order to accomplish the eternal. We must also go to the mountain of the Lord to find our Kingdom calling. As Scripture says, Jesus discussed His death with Moses and Elijah—He looked His destiny right in the eyes and without blinking accepted it. He made Himself *available* to be overshadowed. Just as Jesus made Himself available to God and was transformed on the mountain, so too we all need a similar mountain-top meeting with the Most High to prepare us to carry out our purpose.

After this encounter, Jesus walked out His eternal purpose with a firm determination—as the Scripture says,

"He steadfastly set His face" (Luke 9:51, *NKJV*). A face-to-face meeting with your eternal purpose will forever alter your perspective. What might previously have seemed overwhelming will now become an overshadowing.

The Source of the Shadow

I understand that a woman like Kerri, who has lived and suffered under the oppressive hand of the enemy, may not readily understand or accept the freedom and joy of being overshadowed. If someone is overshadowed by past pain or present discouragement, it might seem a bit overwhelming to purposely choose to sit under another shadow. Although oppressive circumstances cast discouraging shadows upon our lives, we must stay clear about which kingdom is their source. The difference between overshadowing and oppression lies in the source of the shadow.

To understand the spirit world, we need both to recognize the common spiritual origin of angels and demons and to discern the radical differences between the kingdom of darkness and the kingdom of light. Scripture teaches that angels are beings created by God. They're called the "host" or "armies of heaven" in Nehemiah 9:6 and Psalm 148:2,5. Other biblical names for angels are "sons of God," "holy ones," "spirits," "watchers," "thrones," "dominions," "principalities," "authorities" and "powers."[1] Eventually, angels who rebelled against God were cast down from heaven, becoming demons.

> And there was a war in heaven. Michael and his angels fought against the dragon, and the dragon and his angels fought back. But he was not strong enough, and they lost their place in heaven. The great dragon was hurled down—that ancient serpent called the devil, or Satan, who leads the whole world astray. He was hurled to the earth, and his angels with him (Rev. 12:7-9).

Although the fallen angels were renamed demons following their expulsion from heaven, they did not lose their angelic powers. As angels, they had been sent to encourage the heirs of salvation. After their fall, their assignment was perverted, and they began to use their abilities to serve the kingdom of darkness. Rather than picking up words of life sent forth in faith and carrying them to their furthest good, they pick up negative words rooted in doubt and carry them to their most harmful end. Those spirits, who were once holy messengers, are now used by the enemy for his destructive purposes. Demonic oppression is the hovering of spiritual darkness over us, sent to destroy us, to keep us down and under the cover of that darkness (see Matt. 6:23; also Job 10:22; 12:25).

Although we cannot escape this ancient struggle for power between the light and the darkness, God did not leave us defenseless against the enemy. He gave us the power and anointing to fight the dark shadow of oppression.

> God anointed Jesus of Nazareth with the Holy Sprit and with power, who went about doing good and healing all who were oppressed by the devil, for God was with Him (Acts 10:38, *NKJV*).

Jesus healed all who were oppressed by the devil, and we are commissioned to do the same. Oppression cannot exist where there is wholeness between God and man. If we are entertaining and welcoming the presence of God through our worship, the enemy is afraid to stay, as he would be the only thing standing in the way of our communion with God. A demon would prefer to flee rather than be placed in the path of an angel. The Scripture testifies to the fact that the oppressive power of the enemy over our lives can be broken through worship.

David would take his harp and play. Then relief would come to Saul; he would feel better, and the evil spirit would leave him (1 Sam. 16:23).

When we worship our way through oppression, we are pressing into the presence of God, positioning ourselves to receive the favor of His overshadowing. In the kingdom of heaven, to be overshadowed means that we have found favor with God!

If we do a word study on the word "overshadow," we find that in every account it denotes a work of the Holy Spirit in response to God's favor. On two separate occasions (see Mark 9:8; Luke 9:34), the word "overshadowed" was used to describe when the Holy Spirit was sent to affirm God's love for His Son, Jesus. At the Mount of Transfiguration, a bright cloud overshadowed the disciples and these words were used: "This is My beloved Son, in whom I am well pleased" (Matt. 17:5, *NKJV*).

But perhaps the most memorable usage of the word "overshadow" was in the angelic announcement to Mary, the young virgin who would become the mother of Jesus.

The angel went to her and said, "Greetings, you who are highly favored! The Lord is with you." Mary was greatly troubled at his words and wondered what kind of greeting this might be. But the angel said to her, "Do not be afraid, Mary, you have found favor with God. You will be with child and give birth to a son, and you are to give him the name Jesus. He will be great and will be called the Son of the Most High. The Lord God will give him the throne of his father David, and he will reign over the house of Jacob forever; his kingdom will never end." "How will this be," Mary asked the angel, "since I am a virgin?" The angel answered, "The Holy Spirit will come upon you, and the power of the Most High will overshadow you. So the holy one to be born will be called the Son of God" (Luke 1:28-35).

The angel assured Mary that she had found favor with God, so it is clear that she was pleasing to the Lord. I have often wondered what exactly drew God's attention to this young girl. Sadly, it is in our nature to desire instructions on how to "do" something to receive the favor of God. I know that I am not the only woman who wonders about Mary and what made her "the one."

We don't know much about Mary before the angel Gabriel came to her, so all we can study is her responses to the bidding of the Holy Spirit. Fortunately, that is enough to validate the rare spirit of this young Jewish girl. How many of us, when taken completely off guard, would respond with so much grace and humility? Mary's instant response to the angel's amazing announcement tells us a lot about her character and attitude toward God.

The Instant Power of Agreement

If we study the story of Mary and work our way backward from the favor of overshadowing, we find that her instant agreement springs from deep faith. When the angel appeared to Mary, her response was immediate. Mary didn't just stand there and ask if she could have some time to think about this proposal. She could have said, "Let me sleep on it, and I'll get back to you." But she didn't. She simply answered, "May it be to me as you have said" (Luke 1:38).

When we come into agreement with the Spirit of God, making ourselves available, we set our spirit into alignment with the Holy Spirit. Mary's response shows us that instant agreement with God springs from a deeper level of faith than confession alone. Only genuine faith responds with an unwavering yes to God's unknown will.

Even though we don't have an angel in our bedroom as Mary did, once we hear the Word of God, it is required of us to respond. Can you imagine responding as she did? Can you imagine being so aligned in the spirit that you could instantly answer yes without consulting your schedule or agenda?

My prayer in times of busyness has been, "God, give me more time for You." One day it finally dawned on me how rude this request would be if aimed at my husband. What it would essentially say to him is, "You are not as important as the rest of my life, and I am sorry about that. But if I just had one more hour in the day, I would be all yours!" I have discovered that God will not push my mothering, my wifely duties or my writing career to the side to make time in my schedule for Him. What He will do is love me from afar and dream about what will happen between us when I wake up one day and love Him. Sensing His desire for me makes me long to faithfully get on with life so that I have more time for His attention.

How many of us are so busy that we have no room for a creative miracle, no space in our lives for a "new baby"? Why would God chase us down to overshadow us and release us into a new level of "offspring management" when we are overbooked as it is? We should always live with room in our lives for whatever God might have for us—this is what it means to be available to Him. How can we say that we expect divine intervention but plan our lives in such a way that we leave out the divine?

I am talking to the overcommitted here, not the unfaithful. This is not a permission slip to be flaky and undependable. In fact, if we have not proven ourselves faithful in most areas of our lives, we are not qualified to receive the offspring of God. Even Child Protective Services has a standard of stability for parents—how much higher is God's standard when He chooses to entrust part of Himself to us! If we are faithful to what we have been given—talent, opportunity, and so on—then we have given God something to work with on our behalf.

Conceive the Impossible

Returning to the story of Mary's visitation by the angel Gabriel in Luke 1, we see a pivotal statement in verse 37: "For nothing is impossible with God."

I have often wondered if women focus on Mary's virginity as the reason for God's favor and overshadowing. If we focus only on the fact that God needed a virgin, and

Mary met the requirement, then we may miss the message. Although I have no desire to take away from the purity and nobility in Mary's virginity, I would like to direct your attention to an important principle at work here. God needed a virgin—a woman who had not known a man in an intimate, sexual way—so that His seed in her could not be confused with the work of another. God wanted to use this virgin to produce an offspring born of His spirit through her flesh. Virginity was required simply because God wanted to produce an offspring out of an otherwise impossible human situation.

God works in the realm of impossibilities. The same God who makes a virgin a mother wants to create the impossible in us. If you have been abused, misused or soiled by life's relationships, God will call you to speak, breathe and live purity. He works against the natural to conceive the supernatural. If you are a single woman who desires nothing more than to have a family and children but have not yet seen this as a reality, God will use you mightily as a mother to many in spite of your circumstances.

If we can capture the essence of the exchange of worship, we can conceive the truth of God's heart for us. God does not publish His requirements of others He has used in order to make us feel unworthy by comparison. The purpose of our knowing the details is to ignite our faith so that we may believe the impossible the moment we are aware of His desire to use us for His wonderful purpose!

Blessed is she who has believed that what the Lord has said to her will be accomplished! (Luke 1:45).

Mary conceived the will of God the moment she believed His promise. To "conceive" means "to receive the belief," and that is why when we say that something is unbelievable, we also say it is inconceivable. Essentially, to believe is to conceive. They are inseparable. It takes believing faith to conceive the seed of God. Our belief in Him speaks trust beyond knowledge, and He knows when we are ready—when we are ready to receive.

The Aroma of an Open Spirit

My husband surprised me one day by commenting on a scent he sensed coming from my hair, face and breath. He said, "You have that smell again." Thinking that it was a bad thing, I was embarrassed and asked him what the smell was like. When he told me it was like sweet flowers, I was shocked. In fact, the first time he said it, I didn't believe him. Then I asked him what he really wanted, because he had just given me what I considered an extreme compliment. But month after month he would notice and comment on the same scent. After more than 11 years of marriage, we have come to expect this smell as a sign of fertility.

I later found out this fragrance is not all that rare. In fact, it is a result of pheromones being released to signal ovulation. The reason more women are not aware of it is because they cannot smell it on themselves, and a husband must know his wife very well to sense the difference between this unique scent and the scents emanating from the many products and perfumes we women use. But just as God created a little fragrance signaling the readiness of a woman for conception, so too do we give off a unique and fragrant spiritual signal.

Our faith releases a fragrance that draws the heart of God. Overshadowing is God's response to a spirit found open and available to Him. When everything aligns properly in our spirit, we are ripe for conception. We must be found willing, acceptable, vulnerable, broken and available, all at once, in order to respond properly to the Holy Spirit.

Each of these attributes shines through the life of Mary, the mother of Jesus. This chaste and humble young woman showed her willingness through her instant response of faith. Mary's acceptance of the favor of God is a subtle study of her character, as she could have disqualified herself by showing any sign of shame or pride. Although we later learn that, due to her humility, Mary was surprised that God would use a "lowly" girl like herself, her response did not spring from an overblown opinion of herself, but rather from her acceptance of God's sovereign choice. Her emphasis, as ours must be, was on God's greatness, not on her qualifications—or lack thereof.

After hearing the angel's announcement, Mary made herself vulnerable by fearlessly asking how all this would take place. The way in which she asked, "How will this be?" reveals her faith—that she believed the conception would happen, but she didn't understand *how* it would happen. She must have given her life to God long before the angel entered unannounced, for she most surely knew, after hearing what God had planned for her, that she could face being rejected by her family and fiancé, and even risk death by stoning. And yet, disregarding her own inevitable brokenness, Mary welcomed the presence of God with open arms.

Hosting the Holy Spirit

Jesus was ushered into this world by His mother, Mary, and ushered out of it by another Mary—the one who anointed Him for His death. How awesome for two women with the same name to prophetically host the Holy Spirit as He moved them to make way for the Body of Christ. Mary, the mother of Jesus, gave her own body to deliver the Son of God, made of flesh, into this world; when it was time for Jesus to transition back to the Father through death, Mary of Bethany prepared His body for burial. One Mary bore Him, and one Mary buried Him. Although Mary was a popular name at the time, I don't think irony is to blame for this coincidence.

There is a special message here for all women: Jesus was first welcomed into this world by a woman, and when Jesus knew His destiny was death, a woman was the only one to affirm Him through her prophetic gift. I find it reassuring to know that when God wanted His only Son to be welcomed, treasured, nurtured and trained, He sought out a woman to do His will. God could have arranged a royal birth attended by kings and dignitaries, and He could have had His Son reared by a well-respected Senator—but He didn't. He chose a simple, faith-filled woman to bear and raise His only Son.

God entrusted His most valued gift, Jesus, to a woman. Mary, the mother of Jesus, must have had many qualities that God wanted her to pass on to His Son. Furthermore, God trusted Mary to care for, embrace and chasten His Son as He grew. The most important test of a great parenting partnership is agreement. Mary had shown her ability to instantly align herself with the Spirit of God, a divine ability that would have been essential in the upbringing of Jesus.

Yet Mary was not the only woman who figured prominently in Jesus' life. Unlike Jesus' mother, Mary of Bethany's anointing gift had a profound effect upon the life and death of Jesus Christ.

On the surface we see Mary of Bethany as a passionate worshiper who poured her very expensive perfume upon Jesus' feet and then wiped them with her hair. Beyond that was the prophetic gesture her extravagant gift represented. As Jesus was being plotted against, betrayed and patronized by those who missed the meaning of His life, as the disciples were gathered around the table with their heads in matters of politics—Mary was at His feet with her hands, her heart and her hair drenched in the prophetic.

> "Leave her alone," said Jesus. "Why are you bothering her? She has done a beautiful thing to me. . . . She did what she could. She poured perfume on my body beforehand to prepare for my burial" (Mark 14:6,8).

When Mary of Bethany anointed Jesus with oil, she prophetically prepared a path for Him through her worship. While the crowds of people worshiping Jesus perhaps thought they would ultimately follow Him to the palace as King of the Jews, Mary said through her intimate act of worship that she would follow Him to His death.

The perfume Mary used to anoint Jesus was described as expensive, pure spikenard. In fact, a price was put on how much it was worth.

For it might have been sold for more than three hundred denarii and given to the poor (Mark 14:5, *NKJV*).

I find it interesting that the value set on her worship was roughly 10 times the amount received by Judas to betray Jesus. Judas betrayed Jesus for 30 pieces of silver, while Mary worshiped Him extravagantly without counting the cost.

Many times I have pondered the lasting effect Mary's fragrant offering may have had upon Jesus over the last days of His life. In those days baths were rare, and astringent soaps were nonexistent. Only time could have worn away the scent of her sacrifice, but time was something

Jesus did not have. I am therefore quite sure that while He was awaiting trial, Jesus sensed Mary's sacrifice. And when He was beaten on the back with 39 lashes, He inhaled her love for Him. And perhaps after many hours of torture, a fragrance filled His heart with remembrance of why He was dying.

Not only was Jesus covered in oil, but Mary was also anointed for having applied it to Him. When Jesus died to cover sin, He fulfilled His promise to Mary of Bethany, for when she gave a prophetic gift, she received the forgiveness of sins directly from Jesus, even before it was given to the rest of the world. Mary's gift blessed Jesus, but it also made provision for her. Although worship is focused on our extravagant love for Jesus, it will spill over and leave a lingering legacy to all who take in the perfume.

Pouring Your Gift upon the Body of Christ

The day for pouring out anointing did not end with Mary of Bethany. There is an earnest call today for us as women to pour out our gift upon the Body of Christ. We are called and anointed to elevate the Body through our extravagant offering. The Spirit of God is hovering over our openness. We can be the vessels He chooses to use for

His glory. Our lives and every experience we have ever had will become a fragrant and lasting legacy when poured out upon His Body.

Jill Briscoe, one of my favorite speakers, once described what it must have been like for passersby the day of Mary's anointing. As they caught the fragrance on the wind they must have said, "Mmm . . . something's been given!"

> And the house was filled with the fragrance of the perfume (John 12:3).

How wonderful would it be for our houses of worship to be so permeated with the perfume of worship that those passing by would stop to smell the fragrance! It is possible for us to push the boundaries of what may seem wasteful in the eyes of others and yet totally engage our Master through worship. Everything we do in life can be dedicated to God.

There are dynamic women today who, much like Mary of Bethany, worship in an "outside of the box" way. Maybe they don't play the piano or pick up a microphone to sing, but they are extravagant worshipers in the ways they have sacrificially laid down their lives.

Your worship experience has the potential to take you into the future. Women of the Bible who were overshadowed have left legacies and indelible imprints on our lives today. Their worship thousands of years ago still rings out and enters our conversations today.

I long to host the Holy Spirit with the same spirit of humble acceptance shown by Mary, the mother of Jesus, and by Mary of Bethany. We can follow in their footsteps today, since God is not finished birthing offspring of the Spirit. We don't have to be married or in full-time ministry to be used by God to produce greatness for the Kingdom. We only have to be, like the young Jewish virgin, fully willing to accept our calling to conceive the heart of God.

First, however, we must possess the instant response of a heart prepared for overshadowing through willingness, acceptance, vulnerability, brokenness and availability. Overshadowing—the pleasing favor of the Holy Spirit— will produce in us the holy thing we are called to carry and birth, for all the offspring of the "great exchange" are everlasting, multidimensional—and look so very much like their Father!

There is no limit to the legacy of a humble woman who lays down everything and cries out to be overshadowed, and to conceive in complete truth and carry within her the seed of the Most High God.

Sacred Expression

1. How did you feel when you read Kerri's story, including the definition of "submission"?
2. In the past, what did the word "overshadowed" mean to you?
3. What must you do to exchange the source of the shadow from one of oppression to one of power?
4. How can you create an atmosphere of angelic overshadowing?
5. Are you prepared to instantly respond to the Holy Spirit?
6. What humanly impossible thing would you like to receive from God?
7. Do you truly believe that the power of the Most High God will rest upon you?
8. List the holy things (God-given dreams) you have conceived through the power of the Spirit of God.

The Divine Exchange

His Request: No hesitation
Our Reward: To be overshadowed

- Oppression is the enemy's version of *overshadowing*.
- Demons are *fallen angels* who endeavor to cover us with darkness.
- Unholy spirits will not remain in an atmosphere in which they are not being *glorified*. Demons *flee* and angels arrive as a result of our *worship*.
- Instant *agreement* with the Spirit of God brings us into alignment with the kingdom of God.
- Mary's declaration of *"Be it done unto me"* caused her to conceive the impossible.
- My faith releases a *fragrance* that draws the heart of God.
- Mary's faith was based on the *greatness* of God, not on her own *qualifications*.

Meet a Modern-Day Woman of Worship
Ingrid Rosario: "Overshadowed"

One afternoon, as Ingrid looked at the blessing in her life, she asked the Lord, "How did I get here?" She knew that the favor of ministering before thousands around the world and recording a major Spanish album had not come about as the result of her striving or a secret formula for spiritual success. So the question she posed was a good one, born of a heart of gratitude for how far God had brought her.

After asking this question, she recalled something that had happened when she was eight years old. Ingrid had come into the house to find her mother crouched in the corner of the kitchen, crying. Ingrid hurried to find out what was wrong, and she found her mother clutching a wedding invitation addressed to Ingrid and her little brother. However, though this invitation was sent to the children, it was obviously meant for their mother to see, as the invitation clearly specified "NO children."

Now, to understand Ingrid's mother's reaction to this invitation, you must know that Ingrid's parents had been separated for some time. Just recently Ingrid's father had been to the house to visit, and her mother truly hoped they would soon be reconciled. What neither she nor her children knew was that Ingrid's father was already engaged to someone else. The wedding invitation that arrived that day was from his new fiancée.

Years later, this painful memory resurfaced as if in answer to Ingrid's question: "God, how did I get here?" For it was in that memory, at the point that Ingrid realized her daddy was not coming home again, that the vulnerable little girl learned from her mother how to respond to God's plans and purpose, even in the midst of pain.

Ingrid's mother arose from her place of weeping, embraced her confused daughter and put on the audiocassette of a popular Imperials song titled "Praise the Lord," which had been translated into Spanish. Ingrid watched her mother worship and release her anguish as she sang of God's faithfulness in the midst of trials and heartache, and of the great truth that God works through those who praise Him.

God used that memory to show Ingrid that her position as a worshiper began at that moment when her mother chose to respond to her greatest pain and most humiliating loss by worshiping. Ingrid's mother chose to be overshadowed by God—and she passed that legacy along to her daughter.

It wasn't a famous female singer who taught Ingrid what worship was truly about—it was her mother. The path to healing began that day in Ingrid's mother's kitchen. Now, as an adult, Ingrid knew that she had become a worship leader because of a courageous decision her mother had made years earlier. Ingrid was reaping the benefit of a generational thrust toward God. Her mother's act may have been a simple act of worship, but it determined how their little family would respond to the spirit of betrayal that had attempted to permanently derail them. And it was in those years following her father's remarriage that Ingrid found that the only thing that could fill the void created by a missing father was the intimacy she experienced with God during times of worship.

Any of us can worship when it seems as if the world is throwing us a party. It is an altogether different experience when we choose, in a moment of raw pain, to give everything back to God—to be overshadowed by Him. If only we would all run to our heavenly Father when we are wounded, like little girls who have skinned their knees—or been deserted by their earthly fathers—and let Him pick us up, love on us and make us like new! God truly does work through those who praise Him—and He works not only in Ingrid's life, but in yours and mine as well!

Note

1. Wayne Grudem, *Systematic Theology: An Introduction to Biblical Doctrine* (Grand Rapids, MI: Zondervan, 1994), p. 397.

"Divine Declaration"

We were created with the express longing to be overshadowed. But this desire has been met with demonic intention, as the kingdom of darkness seeks to oppress. All over the world, for every generation since the dawn of Eve, women have been oppressed.

There are few countries more oppressive to women than China. Females are regarded as a liability and many times suffer abandonment and a lifetime of neglect. The only thing worse in China than being a female is being a Christian female. But God has not allowed these harsh realities to change His plans for the blessed Chinese people.

Xiao Min was born in Henan, a little village in China. As peasant farmers, her parents were unsure whether they could care for a baby girl. When Xiao Min was about 10 days old, her parents made the heart-wrenching decision to give her away. Curiously enough, a flood came that very day and interrupted their plans.

Her mother and father are now overjoyed that the flood stopped them from making a terrible mistake, for Xiao Min is now a great blessing to her family, as well as to countless others.

As Xiao Min grew, she began to develop severe allergies, causing her to feel dizzy and nauseous. Her health problems eventually caused her to drop out of school while she was still in junior high. Her aunt later invited her to a home church, where she was miraculously healed. Shortly after her healing and salvation, Xiao Min began to hear songs coming from within.

Xiao Min sang her first hymn, given to her by the Holy Spirit, at the end of 1990. Since then there have been more than 900 others. Her songs, which have come to be known as the Canaan Hymns, are sung by over 8 million Chinese believers. No one, including her family, could have guessed that God would use her in such a profound way—especially considering that Xiao Min cannot read or score music and was not able to finish high school.

Many consider Xiao Min's authenticity and humility to be her most memorable attributes. The vast number of Chinese underground believers who now sing her songs make Xiao Min the most celebrated worship leader of our time. The threat of being arrested and spending time in prison because of her faith has only heightened her desire to be used by God in whatever manner would most bless His people. Only God could orchestrate such irony by taking a young girl from the most oppressive of environments and using her to create an atmosphere of hope through worship, not only for China but also for the world!

On any given day in China, female infants are abandoned because of their gender. In Africa, the genitals of infants and young girls are mutilated in tribal religions and in the name of Islam as a first stab of hatred toward their femininity. And in the Middle East, women are literally covered from head to toe, with only their eyes showing, as a sign of their inferior standing in the world.

Though I find myself in America, where certain liberties are understood, I observe a different brand of oppression regarding women. We are blessed, favored, released—and yet we have taken on a learned helplessness to which we are blind. We are held captive not by greed, religious ritual or slavery but by spending, surgery and self-indulgence. I am not saying that seeking to enhance our beauty is wrong; I appreciate beautiful things, as I know God does. What I am saying is that we have been empowered by God to do more with our lives than just look pretty.

I believe that women in America, and in other prosperous parts of the world, are searching for a more purposeful existence. Yet it seems we are searching for the spirit of revelation in the reflection of our own mirrors. This also is oppression, for we are distracted from our calling by our daily pursuit: decorating our lives with things that have no eternal value. When are we going to wake up and see that God has given us a "divine declaration"? We have been freed so that we can set others free.

What an honor and opportunity we have to serve the kingdom of God! We are blessed to have been chosen as ministers of healing to the oppressed. We have not been called, anointed and empowered with authority solely to decorate our own personal lives, but rather we are called to the decoration of nations. All over the world women are in need of freedom from oppression. They are crying out to be overshadowed by the Holy Spirit. They are longing to be used to host the very hope of the Kingdom.

I have seen a vision, a horizon that shines on the freedom of women all over the world. This Holy Spirit sight confirms to me that this oppressive counterfeit "covering" of demonic origin has timed out. Our Creator has set upon us a mandate. We must get over the distracting details of our lives, accept with fervor and passion the divine declaration of our divine opportunity and, acting as many Marys, host the Holy Spirit as He blesses and heals the oppressed.

When Women Worship CD

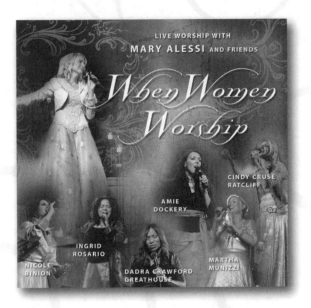

Available in stores and online at
www.whenwomen.com

Check website for
When Women Worship live Event listings!

Also Available in the Best-Selling Worship Series

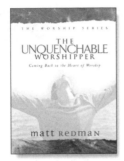

The Unquenchable Worshipper
Coming Back to the Heart of Worship
Matt Redman
ISBN 978.08307.29135

The Heart of Worship Files
Featuring Contributions from Some
of Today's Most Experienced
Lead Worshippers
Matt Redman, General Editor
ISBN 978.08307.32616

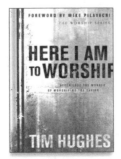

Here I Am to Worship
Never Lose the Wonder
of Worshiping the Savior
Tim Hughes
ISBN 978.08307.33224

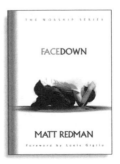

Facedown
When You Face Up to God's Glory, You
Find Yourself Facedown in Worship
Matt Redman
ISBN 978.08307.32463